Exhibit Design 2

Exhibit Design 2
Trade Show Graphics

compiled by **Robert B. Konikow**

PBC International, Inc., New York

Distributors to the trade in the United States:
PBC International, Inc.
One School Street
Glen Cove, NY 11542

Distributors to the trade in Canada:
General Publishing Co. Ltd.
30 Lesmill Road
Don Mills, Ontario M3B 2T6, Canada

*Contact PBC International, Inc. for information
on the distributors throughout the rest of the world.*

Library of Congress Cataloging-in-Publication Data

Konikow, Robert B.
    Exhibit Design 2.

    Includes indexes.
        1. Exhibitions. I. Title. II. Title: Exhibit
design two.
T396.5.K65   1986   659.1'52   85-21825
ISBN: 0-86636-011-5

Color separation, printing, and binding by
Toppan Printing Co. (H.K.) Ltd. Hong Kong

Typesetting by Vera-Reyes, Inc.

PRINTED IN HONG KONG
10 9 8 7 6 5 4 3 2 1

ACKNOWLEDGEMENT

The enthusiasm and participation of all those who submitted material for this book has made *Exhibit Design 2* even more useful and representative than its predecessor. I would like to thank each one of these contributors; their material made this book difficult to put together due to the richness of the entries. The difference between those included and those excluded was sometimes minor, and my decisions were, necessarily, sometimes arbitrary.

Special thanks goes to those designers who were kind enough to let me see their work; and to those professionals in the exhibit industry who prepared the brief essays which appear in the appendix.

Finally, I would like to thank my publisher and their staff for shaping the mass of material and giving it a coherent visual organization.

Robert B. Konikow

Publisher:	Herb Taylor
Project Director:	Cora Taylor
Editor:	Carol Denby
Editorial Assistant:	Carolyn Edwins
Art Director:	Richard Liu
Art Associates:	Dan Larkin
	Marilyn Allensbach

Table of Contents

FOREWORD

How much does design contribute to the success of a trade show or educational exhibit? It is certain that *bad* exhibit design can seriously compromise the goals of an exhibitor. A design that is expensive to construct or is complicated or time-consuming to set up is impractical. However, a design that is simple to set up, has a logical traffic pattern, and involves practical use of space, simple materials and construction techniques, may not be attractive to passersby. Exhibit designers who overlook the most basic principles of exhibit design can create a booth that's the focal point of a show; however, it will likely fall short of the exhibitor's overall goal.

What is the definition of ''good'' or ''bad'' design? Are there standards for judging whether or not an exhibit is ''well-designed?'' When we look at the purpose of an exhibit—any exhibit—we may find some answers.

Any exhibit, whether large or small, dramatic or subdued, must work. It must create a business-like setting, communicate the overall image of the exhibiting company and it must satisfy the overall objectives of the exhibitor.

Simply stated, design is just one of the building blocks that makes an exhibit successful; it should never be regarded as the only element of a successful exhibit.

A good exhibit designer must play a variety of roles in the development of the exhibit. First, the objectives of the exhibitor must be understood. If those objectives are unclear, or perhaps undefined, the designer should help define those objectives by asking all the right questions, and by knowing how to interpret the answers.

A good designer must also be willing to devote some time and energy to learn as much as possible about the client's business, products, markets, competition, and marketing strategies. Good exhibit design supports the total company, not just one small segment.

Also, a good exhibit designer must get inside the client's mind, to ferret out the needs, objectives and messages that should be integral to the design.

To answer the initial question, design *does* play a role in successful exhibiting. It is neither the beginning nor the end, but another link in the chain that ties together the total effort.

This book contains many exhibits; some good, some better, and some excellent examples of design which support the marketing goals of the exhibitor.

Hopefully, these ideas will help spark new ideas that will make your next exhibit more successful.

Martha B. Wolf
McDonald Moving Services,
Raynham, Massachusetts
Past President, The International
Exhibitors Association

INTRODUCTION

Exhibit design should be significantly more than just filling space. A work of art is not required to function in a commercial environment, but to stand on its own. This is not true of an exhibit. To succeed, its design must directly support the marketing objectives of the project. Without this support, the exhibit functions as a piece of art, but not as a marketing tool.

If a new company produces high-technology products that compete with those of established firms, a frivolous or overly intricate exhibit may be counter-productive. If the designer is told, "We need excitement; a gimmick to draw people in," the resulting design may better be characterized as a sideshow or an art exhibit, rather than as a marketing tool. An elephant and palm trees at a computer show may call attention to the exhibit, but for all the wrong reasons. Simple, creative design that builds credibility and projects a feeling of technical competence would serve the new company better.

Designers and those who commission them should remember these important criteria:

- The effectiveness of an exhibit is directly proportional to the quality of input used to develop the design.

- The use of gimmicks in trade show exhibits is often directly related to the absence of clear marketing goals or a coherent selling strategy.

- It is better to create a positive selling atmosphere than an exciting design atmosphere.

Successful design solutions go beyond building the right atmosphere and projecting the correct image. They share many of the characteristics of an art exhibit:

- They are people-oriented in that they provide sufficient space for visitors to move around.

- They communicate a theme that supports the client's marketing objectives.

- They offer an inviting, visually simple appearance.

- They strive to communicate with predetermined target groups within the overall audience of trade show attendees.

- They do not intimidate or confuse visitors.

- Their contents relate to specific products or services being sold by the exhibitor.

- They clearly identify the exhibitor.

- They leave show visitors with a positive, informed impression of the exhibitor and the exhibitor's products or services.

- They are not created to achieve "a look," but to help attain marketing objectives and support a company's image.

The best way to ensure that the design process results in a marketing-oriented exhibit is to start with the fundamentals: a marketing plan or sales strategy. Three important elements are:

- The design team should be involved in all planning meetings from the conception of the project on.

- Aim the design at the target audience. The designers should know who these groups are and should be given as much information as possible about them.

- The design must accommodate all of the functions needed to support the

exhibitor's marketing objectives. If the objectives are compromised for an exhibit's "look," the results will also be compromised. Many good designs are compromised before they reach the exhibit floor because their role as a support to the marketing objectives wasn't sufficiently considered.

Successful exhibit design requires a blending of space planning, product design and graphics, and an understanding of structure and materials.

With these requirements, exhibit design is best left to professionals whose specialty is the trade show medium. Exhibition at trade shows can be a powerful selling tool, but fulfilling that potential is dependent on a clear understanding and support of sound marketing objectives.

George G. Dorr, President
Giltspur Exhibits
Rochester, New York

Chapter **1**

Techniques of Exhibit Design

At first glance, it may seem a long distance artistically from the couteur salons of New York and Paris to the trade exhibits of the New York Coliseum or the Paris Air Show. Yet the challenge faced by the exhibit designer is, in many ways, similar to that confronting the fashion designer at the close of a season: Everyone knows that next year's line will feature pants, skirts, dresses, and shirts; everyone knows the models will be tall and painfuly thin. But only the designer's genius can transform these familiar shapes into a unique, provocative fashion statement.

This chapter highlights some of the original ways exhibit designers have found to energize familiar elements. The first step to an imaginative—and effective—exhibit is to form a strong partnership with the client. Exhibit design isn't an individual sport. It's a team effort that must include the client's marketing, sales, and public relations representatives, experienced and talented designers, and detail-oriented producers. The qualifications to carry out the proposed program successfully include knowledge, skill, facilities, and other resources necessary for an effective exhibit design.

These exhibits demonstrate some of the original techniques used by exhibit designers to create imaginative and effective displays.

Modular Displays

Few exhibitors—particularly small companies—can bear the cost of a new exhibit for each trade show they attend. Modular displays can be an efficient solution because they can be easily adapted to spaces of different sizes and shapes.

These versatile series of modules may be freestanding or connected in more than one configuration. Perhaps more attractive to the cost-conscious designer is that modular units can be customized to a particular audience through the use of interchangeable graphic panels, headers and signs. Velcro used as a wall covering helps make these simple changes even easier.

For exhibitors with limited budgets, it's also possible to use modules as building blocks, constructing additional modules (and increasing the size of the exhibit) as money becomes available.

Modular components also enable the designer to adapt his creation to design regulations stipulated by various show sponsors. Parts of the exhibit that don't meet the more stringent rules imposed by other shows—such as tall canopies, towers, and riser platforms—can be omitted from the design.

Such novelties as tall canopies, towers, and riser platforms can be added or omitted from a display depending on the rules imposed by the individual exhibit show. Designed by Bill Moss.

The varied use of stretched canvas shown in this exhibit designed by Bill Moss is a real attention-getter. It can be used to either enclose or increase existing booth space — economically.

This exhibit, designed by Armando Orubeondo for Sysgen, is a good example of an exhibitor using modules as building blocks. The exhibit is in its third stage of development.

VISUALS

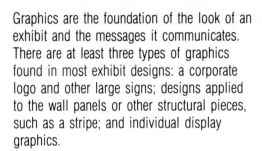

Graphics are the foundation of the look of an exhibit and the messages it communicates. There are at least three types of graphics found in most exhibit designs: a corporate logo and other large signs; designs applied to the wall panels or other structural pieces, such as a stripe; and individual display graphics.

Photographs are often inexpensive large-scale graphics. The 3M Scanamural process is a relatively new development that is both cost effective and attractive. A scanner reads a photograph, which is then significantly enlarged by a computer-controlled airbrush. These graphics make it easy to alter the look or an exhibit frequently with minimal expense. One exhibitor painted the Scanamurals on canvas, which were then stretched onto a wood frame. The entire exhibit could be rolled up and shipped very economically.

Another unique graphic technique is the "moving message" LED display board. Controlled by a microprocessor, they can be pre-programmed to display one message, or messages can be programmed on-site. When supported by a large tower or hung from the second floor of a double-deck exhibit, these message boards promote not only the exhibitor's name and location, but also the times of demonstrations, show events sponsored by the exhibitor, and names of contest winners.

Screenprinting on vinyl wall fabric, applied directly to the wall, results in a very durable and even washable display for Diesel Construction, designed by Gene Lindman.

These high-contrast photographs are black & white prints given a solid color dye wash, created by designer Gene Lindman for Talman Saving & Loan. Custom colors are achieved at a cost well below screenprinting.

This exhibit, produced by Shotel for Centennial Computer Corporation, graphically displays a central tower bearing the company name on its three extended arms. Strategically placed illuminated panels tell the story of software.

The Product as the Exhibit

Sometimes the best way to display a product is to make the product the display. For Continental Can, the most effective way to showcase a new type of can was to build a plexiglass platform supported by 15,000 of the new cans.

The use of the product as the exhibit is particularly appropriate for makers of building materials and manufacturers of exhibition structures. A forest products conglomerate used its plywoods and veneers as wall panels, for example. One exhibit systems company incorporated one of each type of unit it builds into its exhibit, including a 20-foot overhead bridge.

Giant replicas of other types of products can also attract attention, but this much-used technique needs a unique twist in order to be effective. Pentel's "blow-ups" of ordinary office supplies—a pen the size of a baseball bat—are unexpected and therefore eye-catching.

If used as the focal point of the exhibit, products may need an appropriate background. Freightliner Trucks used a replica of a highway off-ramp as the right setting for actual trucks, thus transporting the viewer into a visualization of the products in use.

For Continental Can, the most effective way to showcase a new type of can was to build a plexiglass platform supported by 15,000 of the new cans. Designed by Ron Ferguson.

Designed by Omnicom Ltd., Pentel's "blow-ups" of ordinary office supplies — a pen the size of a baseball bat — are unexpected and therefore eye-catching.

This exhibit, designed by Bruce Backer of Exponents, displays its own products using almost every design element it offers.

A Place for Everything

Product, stationery, coats, hats, contracts, order forms, business cards, message pads, and sales literature—the variety and number of things that need to be kept out of sight within the exhibit booth seem endless. One solution, of course, is to include a storage room within the exhibit area, such as that used by the Boorum & Pease Company. In larger exhibits, consolidating storage spaces into one central area makes some sense. It gathers all the extra materials together, making them easy for booth personnel to retrieve.

In smaller exhibits, devoting valuable display space to storage isn't usually cost effective. Instead, many designers strive to integrate strorage into "dead" space under, behind, or inside of other exhibit structures. Many small companies wrap a six-foot table with an apron for quick storage space. But there are other attractive ways to get the most out of a display unit.

For ADAC Laboratories, designers used the bases supporting a cantilever superstructure for storage. Designers for McGard wanted a 12-foot tower in the center of the booth; to reclaim some useable space from the area it occupied, the hollow base was used for storage. Similarly, a cantilevered ceiling was used by General Electric to free work area inside the booth. Computer support equipment was placed in the loft created by the ceiling, getting it out of the way, but leaving it accessible for hands-on demonstrations.

This walk-through exhibit, designed for Boorum & Pease by Impact Exhibits, solves the problem of storage by including a storage room within the exhibit itself.

For ADAC Laboratories, produced by Formetrics, a more attractive way to get the most out of the display unit was to use the bases supporting the large cantilever superstructure for storage.

Produced by Display Presentations for Grumman Data Systems, this exhibitor makes good use of "dead" space. The round pillar on the right offers a video presentation to passersby, while at the same time is used for storage.

THEMES

Visual themes, echoed in the graphic and structural elements of the exhibit, can quickly identify the exhibitor's offerings and can provide the "hook" to unify the display. A theme can be simple and relate directly to the products on display. TRW Williams chose to showcase its tools in a high-tech setting reminiscent of an industrial shop. Brushed aluminum, exposed bolts, and shop lights helped convey the impression. For a line of natural food products, designers recreated the look of an old-fashion country grocery. The colors and shapes, as well as the suggestion of "old-time goodness," fit well with the graphics and product packaging. Similarly, the open greenhouse structure constructed for Care Free Garden instantly identified the product line.

A theme may also be chosen to help attract a select audience. For Manville, a building products company, designers used truss-like structures to appeal to architects and builders. Other designers chose themes that made a statement about the company's product line. To dispel the myth that suntan lotions are summertime items, Suntana mounted a display with panels depicting the four seasons.

Museum and other educational displays often make good use of themes, and may be a good source of inspiration for commercial designers. A ski museum located in a ski lodge restaurant, Cafe Kandahar, demonstrates an effective theme presentation. At the Iron Range Interpretive Center, a turn-of-the-century saloon furnished ample thematic material for displays that described lifestyles of the period.

Designed by Omnicom Ltd. for Care Free Garden Products, the skeleton greenhouse calls attention to the nature of this exhibitor's products, easily identifying the product line.

Exhibits for this unusual combination museum/restaurant, designed by Design Dynamics for Cafe Kandahar, demonstrate an inspirational and effective theme presentation.

TRW Williams chose to showcase its tools in a high-tech setting reminiscent of an industrial shop. Designed by Jack Snyder, this exhibit is made of brushed aluminum, exposed bolts, and industrial shop lights.

Unique Ideas

For the visitor walking the aisles of a trade show, turning a corner and encountering an exhibit that's truly extraordinary comes like a cool drink of creativity in the desert of ordinary commercial displays. It's impossible to define or categorize these displays simply because they are unique, one-of-a-kind ideas.

Certainly, for visitors to the Louisiana World's Fair, the U.S. Army Corps of Engineer's display—built inside of a huge dredging barge—was unexpected. Viewers roaming the aisles of the Pacific Science Center in Seattle, Washington, must have been equally surprised when, mixed in among the graphic panels detailing 7,000 years of Chinese history, they found actual craftsmen demonstrating their arts.

The element of surprise can be gained by displaying unusual or overwhelming objects. Black & Decker displayed an automobile sawed in half, dramatically showcasing automotive parts. NCR created a replica of a computer assembly, enlarged 700 times, while a rear projection screen carried graphics explaining in detail how the unit works.

Sometimes, the unusual is in the method of presentation. Esprit's colorful, avant garde clothing display featured racks of clothing mounted on wire grid panels that moved on an overhead trolley track. The panels allowed sales personnel to work with two buyers simultaneously, with privacy provided by Levolor blinds. For Microma watches, designers mounted samples on mannequins attached to the exhibit's walls. Pin spots illuminated the watches, leaving the mannequins as shadowy background figures.

The U.S. Army Corps of Engineers brought a Mississippi dredge out of retirement to house the story of the Corps and the river for the Louisiana World's Fair,

The product was the new liquid crystal display watch for Microma and rather than use display cases, the designer obtained custom mannequins that were mounted on the back wall.

Chapter 2

Small Exhibits

Less than 400 square feet/
37 square meters

Pity the small exhibitor. Faced with limited budgets and exhibit space, he must compete with larger, more prominent companies for the attention of passersby. But small can be beautiful—and effective—as you'll see in the entries contained in this chapter.

The exhibit designs displayed in this chapter share some common features. All are contained in less than 400 square feet. Most of the exhibits are based on a single, dynamic theme which is supported with the appropriate construction materials, graphics, lighting, and display units. And nearly all the featured exhibits are versatile, allowing the exhibitor to adapt them to a variety of sales presentations and trade shows.

Beyond these similarities, each design offers a unique approach to communicating the small exhibitor's marketing objectives. An efficient use of space has enabled some designers to include demonstration stations, conference areas and storage space. Others use striking graphics to attract business prospects—12-ft. towers, illuminated three-dimensional logos, and large headers positioned over a slightly raised conference area—while other exhibits feature unusual shapes that contrast with the horizontal and vertical lines common to most exhibits.

Aside from visual and structural considerations, the small exhibit must showcase the company's product line. Unfortunately, many small exhibitors—often new companies—seek to create awareness for their goods by crowding the small space with product, sales personnel, product literature, and huge blow-ups of the corporate logo. As a result, the design elements compete for attention, instead of contributing to a central theme. In working with the small company, the designer must carefully select materials that are essential to the design, not merely those which are convenient for the exhibitor.

Exhibitor: TRW Williams
Designer: Jack Snyder
Producer: Design for Industry, Inc., Buffalo,
              New York

In contrast to the usual pegboard-backed tool exhibit, this set-up uses dramatic photos of tools specific to an industry, and displays them in a high-tech setting, with brushed aluminum, exposed bolts, and industrial shop lights clamped to a truss-like structure.

Exhibitor: Moog Incorporated
Designer: Jack Snyder
Producer: Design for Industry, Inc., Buffalo,
              New York

The exhibit is made up of modular components, each
with an equilateral triangle cross-section. The sides are
different, one being brushed aluminum with the corporate
ID, the second gloss Formica, and the third a
rear-illuminated matte laminate print film. By turning the
pylons, the appearance can be easily and rapidly changed
to suit the specific market.

Exhibitor: Cooper Bearing Corporation
Designer: Teddie Ryan
Producer: Beyond Exhibits, Inc., Newport News,
              Virginia

Made of modular units, this customized exhibit can take
on many configurations. The graphics and the case units
can easily be replaced to target a different market
segment.

Exhibitor: Amfac Hotels & Resorts
Designer: Gary Artzt
Producer: Freeman Design/Display Company,
Dallas, Texas

This refurbished exhibit includes backlighted
transparencies highlighting the chain's services.

Exhibitor: Naturalite
Designer: Jon Gunderson
Producer: Freeman Design/Display Company,
Dallas, Texas

The feeling of the product, skylights, is carried out in the
booth structure itself, while transparencies show actual
installations. The light boxes can be turned on all at
once, or on and off in sequence.

Exhibitor: Koppers
Designer: Cindie Squilla
Producer: Giltspur Exhibits/Pittsburgh, Pittsburgh, Pennsylvania

The graphic elements are cut out of $\frac{1}{4}$-inch Masonite and mounted on the panels which have a glossy black laminated surface. The cut-outs help to tie in the graphics with the three-dimensional logo.

Exhibitor: Microma
Designer: Steinhilber, Deutsch & Gard, Inc.
Producer: Exhibitgroup San Francisco

The product was the new liquid crystal display watch, and rather than use display cases, the designer obtained custom mannequins that were mounted on the back wall. Pin-spot lights were focused on the wrist watches, both highlighting the product and furnishing the strong light needed to properly read the dials. In addition, the entire line was displayed on a free-floating bar, situated at a good height for inspection, but secure from pilferage.

Exhibitor: Brainerd Manufacturing Company
Designer: Convention Exhibits, Inc., Chicago, Illinois
Producer: Convention Exhibits, Inc., Chicago, Illinois

Three 10 ft. units, all self-packed, make up this 30 ft. display, but each of the two outside units can be used separately. The pegboard back panels accommodate any selection of products, most of them designed for rack display in retail outlets.

Exhibitor: Texize Division, Morton Thiokol, Inc.
Designer: Sugar Creek Studios, Atlanta, Georgia
Producer: Sugar Creek Studios, Atlanta, Georgia

Bent aluminum extrusions and white acrylic make up the curved backwall units, which glow from rear illumination. Transparencies float on its surface.

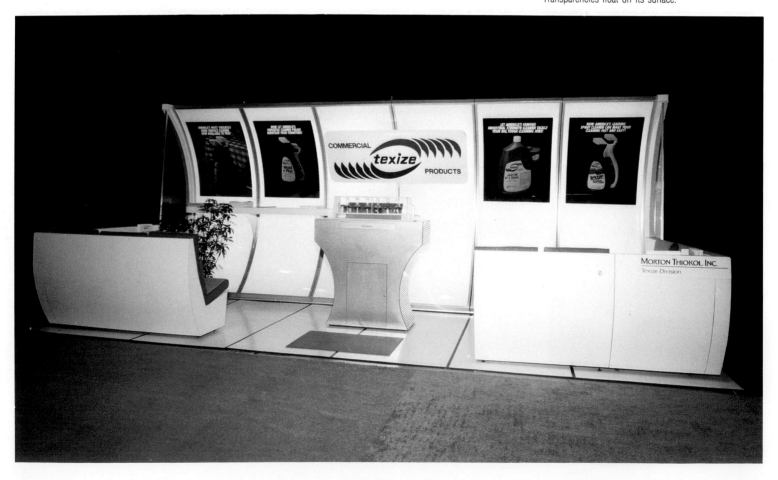

Exhibitor: Pittsburgh Paints
Designer: Mark Noremberg
Producer: Cyclonics Inc., Medina, Ohio

The illusion of pouring paint, with the prominent, colorful logo, was a real show stopper.

Exhibitor: Graber Industries
Designer: The Derse Company, Milwaukee,
                Wisconsin
Producer: The Derse Company, Milwaukee,
                Wisconsin

The product itself is the display, in this simple structure that concentrates attention on the product.

Exhibitor:	Pennwalt/Adapin
Designer:	Raymond J. Crouch
Producer:	Giltpur Exhibits/Rochester, Rochester, New York

To get a low-cost exhibit, the designer combined a custom-built pagoda and existing modular unit. Large silk-screened banners attracted attention from the aisles and highlighted an origami artist in the center of the display.

Exhibitor:	McNeil Consumer Products
Designer:	Holker & Barry, Inc., Brooklyn, New York
Producer:	Holker & Barry, Inc., Brooklyn, New York

Molding the modules of fiberglass allowed the color to be an integral part of the material and avoided painted surfaces. The large transparencies are easily removed from the front of the exhibit, and since no tools are required to change them, labor costs are minimized.

Exhibitor: Graphic Controls
Designer: Thomas G. MacAllister
Producer: Giltspur Exhibits/Rochester, Rochester, New York

Strong graphics and a large, three-dimensional illuminated logo give this 20 ft. backwall exhibit a strong impact.

Exhibitor: McGraw Respiratory
Designer: Convention Exhibits, Inc., Chicago, Illinois
Producer: Convention Exhibits, Inc., Chicago, Illinois

Tubes of plexiglass, edge-lighted from the rear, call attention to the equipment which immediately identifies the situation the product on exhibit is used in. The three-plane transparency on the right serves as an unusual eye-catcher.

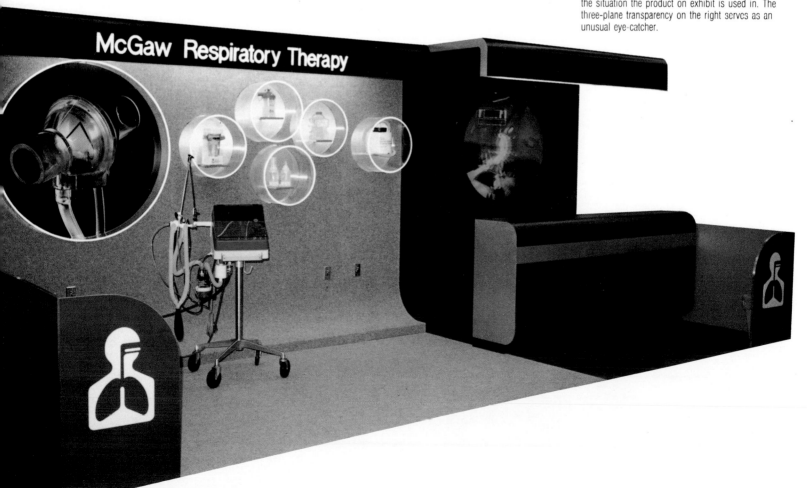

Exhibitor: Personal Performance Consultants
Designer: Michael M. Smit & Associates, Inc.
Producer: Pingel Displays Incorporated,
Saint Louis, Missouri

Covering 200 sq. ft., this 20 ft. backwall, modular exhibit may be used as separate 10 ft. exhibits. The warm, inviting look of this exhibit is achieved by the use of wood tambour, architectural wall carpeting, and laminates. Information is relayed through the use of Audio-Visual presentations and graphics.

Exhibitor: International Computers, Ltd.
Designer: H & P Associates, Ltd.
Producer: Newton Display Group Ltd., Manchester, England

This island exhibit uses four tubular arches, one in each corner, to support the square header, from which canopies and lights are suspended. The corners are used for the reception desk and conference areas.

Exhibitor: Southwestern Bell Telephone
Designer: Pingel Displays Incorporated
Producer: Pingel Displays Incorporated
Saint Louis, Missouri

The 30 ft. modular backwall exhibit covers 300 sq. ft.
A ten foot module houses three phase revolving graphics;
a five foot module at the right contains a 25 ft. monitor
and interactive laser disc player. Bookend modules
contain 30×40 ft. transparencies, creating a warm,
inviting ambience for hi-tech service presentations.

Exhibitor: LDX Telcom Services
Designer: Pingel Displays Incorporated
Producer: Pingel Displays Incorporated,
Saint Louis, Missouri

The combination of high pressure laminates, metallics,
and corporate accent color are used to achieve the
hi-tech look of this exhibit. Covering 800 sq. ft., with a
20×20 ft. island, the center tower housing equipment
rises 14 ft. for high floor visibility. A small open
conference room adjoins the tower for informal meetings.
The exhibit also contains three zoned divisional meeting
areas plus seating for Audio-Visual presentations.

Exhibitor: Canaan Computer
Designer: Beauregard Corporation, Manchester, Connecticut
Producer: Beauregard Corporation, Manchester, Connecticut

Within this small area was a qualification module, which helped determine the special interests of visitors, and three demonstration modules, one for each of the separate environments and configurations of the computer system being promoted.

Exhibitor: Actrix
Designers: T. Swain, David Jakel
Producer: Formetrics Inc., San Jose, California

To combine sophistication with pizazz, the designer used rich materials integrated with dramatic lighting and visual effects.

Exhibitor: Nashua Corporation
Designer: O'Keefe Design Associates, Inc.,
              Worcester, Massachusetts
Producer: O'Keefe Design Associates, Inc.,
              Worcester, Massachusetts

Designed to mark the entry of the exhibitor into the retail market, the graphics echoed the company's new corporate logo and its package design. The rotating case showed store display pieces. The platform at the rear was used for the appearance of a former professional basketball star, now a memory expert.

Exhibitor: Texas Instruments
Designer: David Nau
Producer: Exponents Inc., San Diego, California

The client requested two identical 20×20 ft. island exhibits, each configurable to 10×60 ft. linear booths. A sophisticated image and 32 ft. of counter space were required. The Exponents system met all these needs, and at a low budget. Visibility was achieved with a 12 ft. tower.

Exhibitor: Vitamaster
Designer: Pingel Displays Incorporated
Producer: Pingel Displays Incorporated,
             Saint Louis, Missouri

This 50×50 ft. island exhibit, covering 2,500 sq. ft., uses a contemporary mono-chromatic color scheme as the background for this state-of-the-art exercise equipment. There are two conference rooms, connected by a 30 ft. logo graphic, and two stages for live product demonstrations, plus two Audio-Visual cabinets. Four double-sided display modules are used for zoning the various product lines.

Vitamaster

Exhibitor: Suntana
Designer: Pingel Displays, Inc., St. Louis, Missouri
Producer: Pingel Displays, Inc., St. Louis, Missouri

Of the three modular units in this exhibit, the two outside ones have panels symbolizing the four seasons, all of which are times when the product on display can be used. The blue of the actual unit, demonstrated on a raised platform, is picked up in the header. The central section, with a large transparency and a moving message, is emphasized by the central white section of the custom carpet.

Exhibitor: Suntana Sunsystems
Designer: Pingel Displays Incorporated
Producer: Pingel Displays Incorporated
                Saint Louis, Missouri

This 600 sq. ft. exhibit was originally designed as a modular 30 ft. backwall exhibit, using trapunto pastels to convey the message that this product may be used any season. An informative electronic moving message was used in the center module. The exhibit has recently been enlarged to contain a conference room, two Audio-Visual presentations, and two additional product display areas. A large revolving graphic was added for greater visibility. The exhibit still maintains modular inline capabilities.

Exhibitor: Door-Oliver, Inc.
Designer: Lopez-Fabrega Design
Producer: Beauregard Corporation, Manchester, Connecticut

The challenge of this exhibit was to incorporate four separate rear projection units in a comparatively small space.

Exhibitor: Chrysler Corporation
Designer: Ken Jamieson
Producer: George P. Johnson Company, Warren, Michigan

Aluminum strips mounted horizontally on the concave surface accent the aerodynamic styling of the car. Twelve concealed strobe lights, timed to go off in split second sequence, flash from left to right. Reflected in each facet, they give the effect of the car traveling at high speed.

Exhibitor: Grumman Data Systems
Designers: Bob Koenigsberg, Ann Listing
Producer: Display Presentations, Farmingdale, New York

Strong graphics catch the eye, and the wood tones offer a congenial atmosphere. The round pillar on the right offers a video demonstration to passers-by, and also has storage space.

Exhibitor: Naval Sea Systems Command
Designer: M. Drue Gillis
Producer: Shotel Inc., Silver Spring, Maryland

The highlight of this exhibit is a large model of a section of an aircraft carrier.

Exhibitor: Mobil
Designer: M. Van Sickle
Producer: Sparks Exhibits, Pennsauken, New Jersey

Exhibiting in an equipment-oriented industry, but having nothing to sell except its expertise, this company relied on simplicity of design.

Exhibitor: Time Inc.
Designer: Robert Blattner Design & Associates Inc.
Producer: Structural Displays, Inc., Long Island
              City, New York

Designed to project the exhibitor's corporate image, and
to be used on behalf of its many divisions, the headers,
the illustrations, and the graphics can easily be changed.
In addition, the central section can stand alone in a 10 ft.
space, while the two wings, together, form another 10 ft.
exhibit.

Exhibitor: Cable Health Network
Designer: Robert Blattner Design & Associates, Inc.
Producer: Structural Displays, Inc.

Designed to give a new company a strong and
sophisticated image, this 20 ft. unit, which can be
adapted to a 10 ft. space, uses large color transparencies,
and a program-viewing unit.

Exhibitor: Boehringer Ingelheim
Designer: Beauregard Corporation, Manchester,
             Connecticut
Producer: Beauregard Corporation, Manchester,
             Connecticut

This simple unit, with its sculpted look, reflects the
image of an aggressive and first-rate pharmaceutical
company. The same structure can fit a 10 ft. backwall
space, as well as this island format.

Exhibitor: Apt Display
Designer: Apt Display
Producer: Nimlok, Morton Grove, Illinois

This unusual shape, which contrasts with the more common horizontal and vertical lines of most displays, catches the eye. Note the scale model of the shelf inside the transparent cube.

Exhibitor: International Shared Services
Designer: Brian Charters
Producer: Design for Industry, Inc., Buffalo, New York

The exhibitor, a bio-engineering service company, selling to high levels of hospital management, needed a location that would give a high-quality, warm, consultative atmosphere, where quiet conferences could take place.

Exhibitor: Hercules Inc.
Designer: Van Sickle & Rolleri
Producer: Display Arts Studios, Inc., New Castle.
              Delaware

In larger show areas, an additional halo backwall and
column are used. The header is of Alucobond, and the
column and backwall are of brushed aluminum.

Exhibitor: Nimlok of England, London, England
Designer: Nimlok of England, London, England
Producer: Nimlok of England, London, England

This unusual exhibit, in which the structure itself is the
product, is designed to permit semi-private conferences
and to discourage casual visitors.

Chapter **3**

Medium Exhibits

401 to 1,600 square feet/
37 to 148 square meters

Exhibits ranging in size from 401 to 1,600 square feet offer the designer more space—and usually a larger budget—to create a striking visual impression. However, a larger area in which to include product displays, demonstration areas, conference rooms, audio-visual presentations, and enlarged graphics puts a greater emphasis on traffic flow and on integrating each design element into a unified marketing concept.

Unlike their smaller counterparts, the exhibits included in this chapter aren't necessarily designed around a central theme. Rather, a variety of design elements and more than one exhibitor may be housed in one, four-to eight-booth exhibit. As for smaller displays, though, finances aren't unlimited, and the designer must choose construction materials that can be reused at other trade shows, or broken down into smaller units for other sales presentations.

This chapter illustrates the variety of approaches that can be taken to minimize congestion and still provide ample space for product demonstrations, audio-visual presentations, workstations, and conference areas. Many feature modular units that can be rearranged for other booth configurations, or used separately in smaller exhibit spaces. You'll find a handsome array of unique design techniques: canopies, expansive back-lit walls, trusses, overhead bridges, towers, spanning headers, two-story exhibits, and sequential base lighting.

Consider, for example, a stage platform supported by 15,000 cans, or a magician performing in front of a large, three-dimensional logo. Some exhibits include inflatable props, while others feature major appliances.

It appears that the designers of these exhibit spaces were limited only by their creativity and ingenuity.

Exhibitor: VR/Wesson
Designer: Norman A. Polacheck
Producer: Hartwig Exhibitions, Milwaukee,
              Wisconsin

Huge mock-ups of cutting heads for machine tools calls attention to this space. A semi-private conference room is behind the tinted clear plastic wall on the left.

Exhibitor: Manville
Designer: Design Dynamics, Denver, Colorado
Producer: Design Dynamics, Denver, Colorado

The large truss-like structures were chosen to give the exhibit an avant-garde architectural look, in order to appeal to architects and builders.

Exhibitor: Thermo Electric
Designer: Plub Design Group
Producer: Dimensional Communications, Northvale, New Jersey

The concept of temperature and its control is conveyed by the effective use of color and light — red and blue — in this exhibit. Each device is supported by clear plexiglass for viewing on all sides. The panel system uses Veluma connectors.

Exhibitor: ICI Americas Inc.
Designer: Emil A. Mellow II
Producer: Display Arts Studios, Inc., New Castle, Delaware

Black panels containing all graphics and copy were mounted on black formica sheets. This allowed the material to be changed easily, and added a high-tech look.

Exhibitor: Centennial Computer Corporation
Designer: M. Drue Gillis
Producer: Shotel Inc., Silver Spring, Maryland

A central tower bears the company name on its three extended arms. Strategically placed illuminated panels tell the story of software, while computers allow hands-on experience.

Exhibitor: AT&T Communications
Designers: Don Graeb, George Coholich
Producer: Creative Productions, Pittsburgh,
               Pennsylvania

Modular units lend flexibility to this display, which uses various animation techniques to demonstrate state-of-the-art communications capabilities.

Exhibitor: The Burdick Corporation
Designer: The Derse Company, Racine, Wisconsin
Producer: The Derse Company, Racine, Wisconsin

The high-tech canopy not only ties the units together, but
contributes to the desired impression of a company that
is in the vanguard of progress.

Exhibitor: Steelcase
Designer: Gerry Glinski
Producer: George P. Johnson Company,
Warren, Michigan

Control over the environment was the key to this design. Faced with poor lighting in the hall and a busy ceiling, the designer called for a fabric ceiling and 32 theatrical lights controlled by a dimmer board. The 28×40 ft. exhibit included a closed theater area for an interactive computer-aided design presentation.

Exhibitor: IUS
Designer: Gary Hobstetter
Producer: Formetrics Inc., San Jose, California

The superstructure of square wooden beams, set at an angle, gives this exhibit a unique appearance.

Exhibitor: MECA
Designer: Robert Blattner Design & Associates, Inc.
Producer: Structural Displays, Inc.,
              Long Island City, New York

A variety of free-standing modules make up this exhibit, which can be put together in 10 ft. or 20 ft. in-line configurations, as well as a 20×20 island, or 20×30 and 30×40 ft. peninsula or island areas. There are two enclosed conference areas.

Exhibitor: Burroughs Corporation
Designer: Don Fee
Producer: Exhibit Works, Livonia, Michigan

The problem was that the exhibit was a long way off in Australia, and the flat panels were supplied by the show itself, so how can you be distinctive? The answer was a unifying, overhead structure of PVC tubing, wooden balls that lock them together, and colorful canvas banners slid onto painted conduits. The ten pyramids created distinct conference and demonstration areas.

Exhibitor: Domain Computer
Designer: mmd Werbung u Design, München, West Germany
Producer: mmd Werbung u Design, München, West Germany

The graceful arches are light enough to keep them from interfering with sight lines, but offer enough weight to tie the separate units together and to call attention to the central display.

Exhibitor: Sysgen
Designer: Armando Orubeondo
Producer: Exhibitgroup San Francisco,
San Francisco, California

This is the third stage of a developing exhibit. Following its start as an in-line structure of lumawall panels, it first acquired workstations, spanning headers, and a product highlight tower. Finally, it was given an additional 4 ft. to raise it to a 12 ft. structure that could fill a 30×30 space.

Exhibitor: Intergraph
Designer: mmd Werbung u Design, München,
               West Germany
Producer: mmd Werbung u Design, München,
               West Germany

Several demonstration units have been placed so that
each can be used with a small group without interfering
with others.

Exhibitor: Daisy Systems Corporation
Designer: mmd Werbung u Design, München,
               West Germany
Producer: mmd Werbung u Design, München,
               West Germany

The slick black surface of this structure makes a strong
contrast with the bright yellow carpet. The company
name, placed high on the structure and repeated at eye
level, cannot be missed.

Exhibitor: Delvotec
Designer: mmd Werbung u Design, München,
               West Germany
Producer: mmd Werbung u Design, München,
               West Germany

It isn't often that one sees a diagonal as strong as this in
the layout of a trade show booth. The canopy and the
bright colored floor pattern attract people into and
through the space, and they can't help noticing the
display as they walk.

Exhibitor: Norwich Eaton Pharmaceuticals
Designers: Jack Snyder, Brion Charters
Producer: Design for Industry, Inc.,
               Buffalo, New York

A library of existing graphics, both vertical and
horizontal, was the basis for designing two types of
modules, finished on all sides. Overhead bridges make
the interconnection in various configurations, keeping the
over-all look, regardless of the amount of space used.

Exhibitor:	Olympus/Medical Scopes
Designer:	Raymond J. Crouch
Producer:	Giltspur Exhibits/Rochester, Rochester, New York

This exhibit consists of four 10 ft. modules, each with a different white band on a blue background, which can be installed in any order to form an attractive background. The intertwining bands suggest the fiber optics of the product. Demonstration counters stand before each panel.

Exhibitor:	Syntex Ophthalmics
Designer:	Giltspur Exhibits/Phoenix, Phoenix, Arizona
Producer:	Giltspur Exhibits/Phoenix, Phoenix, Arizona

This simple booth features casual seating and a central distribution area for literature.

Exhibitor: Telecom Canada
Designer: Marc Soifer
Producer: Studio Summit Inc.,
              Laval, Quebec, Canada

The modular units that make up this island exhibit can
satisfy the company's needs with a variety of
configurations. The panels above counter level are all
interchangeable.

Exhibitor: Bell Atlantic
Designer: .   Sparks Exhibits, Pennsauken, New Jersey
Producer: Sparks Exhibits, Pennsauken, New Jersey

Each of the 5 ft. modules in this display includes a
backlighted header, as well as a plexiglass face area to
provide backlighted graphics, audio-visual presentations,
or product showcases. Simple installation is achieved by
packing each module in its own shipping case and
equipping it with hidden, heavy-duty casters.

Exhibitor: Philips
Producer: Pico Art Pty., Ltd., Singapore

What is more logical than designing a round structure to
fill a square space, but how often is it done? Here the
design permits access from each of the four aisles.

Exhibitor: Crothall American
Designer: Emil A. Mellow II
Producer: Display Arts Studios, Inc.,
New Castle, Delaware

This small island display achieves high visibility with its tower of light-weight Abstracta tubing with particle board panels.

Exhibitor: Amerock
Designer: Norman A. Polacheck
Producer: Hartwig Exhibitions,
Milwaukee, Wisconsin

This peninsular space accommodates a massive display of point-of-purchase materials. Behind the identity sign is a 20×10 ft. second-floor conference room.

Exhibitor: La-Z-Boy
Designer: The Derse Company,
               Grand Rapids, Michigan
Producer: The Derse Company,
               Grand Rapids, Michigan

The modular pylons were assembled on site, and connected with silkscreened cloth banners to tie the exhibit together.

Exhibitor: Care Free Garden Products
Designer: Omnicom Ltd., Elk Grove, Illinois
Producer: Omnicom Ltd., Elk Grove, Illinois

The skeleton greenhouse calls immediate attention to the nature of this exhibitor's products. The diagonal placement adds to its impact.

Exhibitor: General Electric Company
Designers: Tom Lemery, Gene Lindman, and Dana
               Thayer Industrial Design
Producer: Global Exhibition Services,
               Brooklyn, New York

Although there are separate modules for transparencies, products, displays, and graphics, the look carries through to lend cohesion to the exhibit.

Exhibitor: Lighting Business Group, General
               Electric Company
Designer: George Moses
Producer: General Exhibits & Displays, Inc.,
               Chicago, Illinois

The glossy, opaque walls which cover much of the perimeter heighten the brilliance of the illuminated interior, and offers good backwalls for the display of point-of-purchase units. The upper level holds five conference areas, a reception area, and additional product display areas. The unit is convertible to a 40×15 foot configuration, also with a double deck.

Exhibitor: 3M United Kingdom
Designer: Firbank Kempster Ltd.
Producer: Newton Display Group, Ltd.,
Manchester, England

The cut-out letters, placed high on the vertical surfaces, form a prominent part of this exhibit. The design features a large amount of space for operating equipment, each clearly identified by departmental signs.

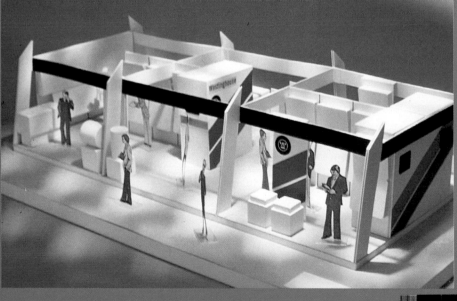

Exhibitor: White Westinghouse
Designer: Don Graeb
Producer: Creative Productions,
Pittsburgh, Pennsylvania

Tall end panels and shorter rear panels permitted the display of a large number of major appliances without overcrowding the space.

Exhibitor: Westinghouse
Designer: Don Graeb
Producer: Creative Productions,
Pittsburgh, Pennsylvania

This exhibit, designed for one of the first international trade shows in China, featured video presentations and a rear illuminated 12 ft. animated landscape of the Great Wall of China.

Exhibitor: American Dermal
Designer: George Post
Producer: Panacom Media Corporation, East
              Brunswick, New Jersey

Demonstration stations are on three sides of this
peninsular space, while the central area, under the
ceiling, can be reserved for one-on-one discussions.

Exhibitor: Bankers Box
Designer: Stuart Stone
Producer: George P. Johnson Company,
              Warren, Michigan

Natural wood and extensive use of plants added warmth
to the area, which included a multi-medium slide
presentation theater. The overhead open truss canopy
supported lighting fixtures that highlighted individual
product islands.

Exhibitor: Lederle Laboratories
Designer: Shlomo Almog
Producer: Holker & Barry Inc., Brooklyn, New York

The columnar units facing the aisles were designed to display large transparencies of product applications. A continuous bronze header connects the columns and makes the exhibit a visual whole. The center columns provide identification from around the hall, and house rear-projection equipment.

Exhibitor: Masterlock
Designer: The Derse Company,
            Milwaukee, Wisconsin
Producer: The Derse Company,
            Milwaukee, Wisconsin

This photo shows just one of the configurations that is possible with this modular exhibit.

Exhibitor: Burroughs Wellcome
Designer: Ralph L. Holker
Producer: Holker & Barry Inc., Brooklyn, New York

Every detail of this coral reef, supporting the theme of 'rediscovery,' is correct. Inside the reef are computer-assisted learning carrels where physicians can test their knowledge of medical subjects.

Exhibitor: Mountain Medical Corporation
Designer: John W. Carveth
Producer: CTI Exhibits, Denver, Colorado

The most notable feature of this exhibit is the special banner system, for an interestingly shaped canopy which gives high impact at low cost.

Exhibitor: Du Pont Company
Designers: Randy Childress, Dennis Van Sickle
Producer: Art Guild Inc.,
West Deptford, New Jersey

This unusual structure made a striking contrast with the more common high-tech approach to the commercial exhibits of a medical meeting.

Exhibitor: Hydrotech Chemical Corporation
Designer: Sugar Creek Studios, Atlanta, Georgia
Producer: Sugar Creek Studios, Atlanta, Georgia

A magician performs in front of the large three-dimensional logo to attract visitors. Two product display counters and transparencies illustrate the product. A conference room in the central structure is enclosed with smoked acrylic.

Exhibitor: Honeywell, Skinner Valve Division
Designer: M. Van Sickle
Producer: Sparks Exhibits, Pennsauken, New Jersey

The feature of this exhibit was an animated fiber-optic map display depicting the company's international manufacturing and distribution network. It also permitted the display of over 75 individual valve products, each of which could be removed for examination or replacement.

Exhibitor: Import Car World
Designer: Michael Grivas
Producer: M. G. Design Associates,
               Chicago, Illinois

Four rectangular arches, each 12 ft. high, 2 ft. square, and 20 ft. across, whose columns held showcases gave dignity and credibility to a young and new company. In the rear is a deluxe, private conference room, with a semi-private conference area on each side. Two simulated gondolas displaying packaged parts formed the background for a central work counter.

Exhibitor: TWA
Designer: John Caulcott
Producer: Impact Inflatables,
Marblehead, Massachusetts

Using an inflatable permits a major impact with little effort in both installation or dismantling. The tail fin is inflated by a powerful air conditioning fan.

Exhibitor: McGard
Designer: David Brace
Producer: David Brace Displays, Inc.,
Alden, New York

Featuring a very small, polished chrome product, this display uses a high gloss, black finish for contrast, with large transparencies of the product. The 12 ft. center column puts the company name in a prominent position, holds a chrome car wheel, showing the product in use, and serves as a storage area. The units, shown here as an island, can be rearranged for an in-line setting.

Exhibitor: Systems Plus
Designer: West and Moravec
Producer: Formetrics Inc., San Jose, California

A monumental tower serves as the eye-catching attraction in this generally open exhibit.

Exhibitor: Cyma
Designer: Curtis Parker
Producer: Formetrics Inc., San Jose, California

The use of units set at an angle not only attracts the viewer's eye because of its unexpectedness, but it also permits larger units under the height regulations.

Exhibitor: Acuson
Designer: M. Adkisson-Bicker
Producer: Formetrics Inc., San Jose, California

The black background of this exhibit is very effective in drawing the attention of the visitor to the exhibit sonographs. The corner pieces delineate the space well without interfering with sight lines or traffic flow.

Chapter **4**

Large Exhibits

1,601 to 4,000 square feet/
149 to 371 square meters

The exhibits featured in this chapter—1,600 to 4,000 square feet in size—must surely be the envy of all small exhibitors. But the extra space and large budgets that play a vital role in the design of large exhibits can pose their own unique set of design challenges. Many of the techniques illustrated in Chapters 2 and 3 are used in these large exhibits, along with some very inventive approaches. Though there's no right way or wrong way to design a large exhibit, one thing is certain: the tougher the struggle with material and audience, the greater the challenge and the potential for innovation.

The designs featured in this chapter are a cornucopia of innovative techniques—an inflatable replica of a pedestrian bridge that stands 20 feet high; a spectacular 20-foot chandelier; massive theaters; multi-level exhibits; a replica of a tropical courtyard;

illuminated roofs; graceful curved walls; and a built-in platform for live entertainment are among a few of the highlights.

Though the design elements differ according to individual products and corporate marketing strategies, nearly all exhibits demonstrate keen attention to organization, no doubt a by-product of lengthy meetings with the client. Esthetics play a vital role in the design process. But perhaps more critical is a design that follows the age-old architectural credo—form follows function.

Not all large exhibits are created for one client. In several examples contained in this chapter, portable panels enabled several divisions of one company to combine marketing efforts. Similar construction materials, such as transparent partitions and plexiglass walls give conference areas an open, airy feeling.

Exhibitor: Allen-A
Designer: Barry M. Hatter
Producer: Alley Shop Inc., Cincinnati, Ohio

This exhibit consists of 10 ft. modular units, each using a 1 in. aluminum tube perimeter form with a honeycomb filler, laminated on the exposed surfaces. The tower unit is used in the larger shows, with the smaller units used later in regional shows or for lobby and in-store displays. Each unit clips together at top and bottom, without the use of tools.

Exhibitor: Brasilianer Schuhverband
Designer: Pinkau-Messbau, Monheim,
West Germany

A detail from a cooperative stand of 16 exhibitors,
occupying 1,938 sq.ft. Meroform elements were used
throughout.

Exhibitor: Kansai Special
Designer: Graphic Displays, Ltd., Staten Island,
              New York
Producer: Graphic Displays, Ltd.,
              Staten Island, New York

Use of the blue carpet edging, which contrasted with the
show's red aisle carpets, delineated this island booth
nicely. The upper-level conference area permitted
preferred prospects to observe any of the machines in
operation from an advantageous viewpoint.

Exhibitor: MJL Industrial Sales
Designer: Graphic Displays, Ltd., Staten Island,
              New York
Producer: Graphic Displays, Ltd.,
              Staten Island, New York

The conference area located above the working area gives
visitors a complete view of machinery at work, while
minimizing the noise level during the demonstration.

Exhibitor: Ecprit de Corp
Designer: Chris Sykes
Producer: Click, Systems Canada, Ltd.,
              Malton, Ontario, Canada

The booth is constructed of 10 ft. wide aluminum framed,
double skin panels, braced diagonally with aircraft wire,
filled with a new, lightweight translucent material made of
extruded polycarbonate.

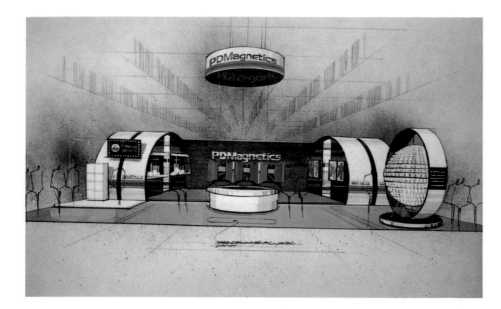

Exhibitor: PD Magnetics
Designer: Mitch Gilbert; Reese, Tomases & Ellick
Producer: The Display House Inc.,
Philadelphia, Pennsylvania

The highlight of this exhibit is the Product Globe, made up of 1,200 video cassette packages mounted on rotating edge-lit plastic discs. This display maximizes awareness of the exhibitor's newly-designed packaging.

Exhibitor: Perkin-Elmer Company
Designer: Robert L. Smith
Producer: Giltspur Exhibits/Pittsburgh,
              Pittsburgh, Pennsylvania

Perkin-Elmer has ten different analytical instruments, but all work through a common computer base. Here, each island unit appeals to a different type of prospect, yet all interact through the computer. Separate island units allow hands-on demos of various instruments.

Exhibitor: Telecommunications Authority of
              Singapore
Designer: Pico Art Pte., Ltd., Singapore
Producer: Pico Art Pte., Ltd., Singapore

To avoid the dullness that might be produced with the limited number of panels and displays, the designer turned to a bright color, topped by an illuminated ceiling.

Exhibitor: NEC
Producer: Pico Art Pte. Ltd., Singapore

In order to accommodate a large number of product lines in the computer and communications fields, the exhibit was segmented into numerous sections, one of which was a live demonstration stage. The extremely large fascia brought prominence to the booth.

Exhibitor: Baldwin-Gegenheimer
Designer: Hans-Joachim Walter
Producer: Display International, Würselen,
              West Germany

The illuminated roof, supported on a special steel structure, was an excellent eye-catcher for the presentation of high-tech products.

Exhibitor: Hewlett-Packard Personal Computer
Division
Designer: Bluepeter, San Francisco, California
Producer: Bluepeter, San Francisco, California

Wanting to change its image from an engineering-oriented company to that of a leader in the personal computer marketplace, the exhibitor asked for an image of strength, without overwhelming the audience, to build its perception as a stable but friendly company. The basic display element used to produce a crisp, clean environment was a classic structure with fluted columns, joined by headers with rear-illuminated corporate identification.

Exhibitor: Xerox
Designer: Raymond J. Crouch
Producer: Giltspur Exhibits/Rochester,
Rochester, New York

Here a story is told in a series of platforms, each on a different level, each representing a different department of a hypothetical company, each showing a different product application. The booth was designed to keep all the action facing toward the center of the booth and away from the distraction of the show floor.

Exhibitor: Altos Computer
Designer: Bluepeter, San Francisco, California
Producer: Bluepeter, San Francisco, California

Pillars, some 8 ft., some 16 ft., topped with 22 in. illuminated spheres, form the dominant element of this display. They are connected by overhead steel truss structures that bear signs. Lighting is used effectively, with the pillar globe motif reflected in smaller spheres on the graphic panels, and fluorescent fixtures, tinted with gels, in every product shelf, resulting in a wash of color on the floor.

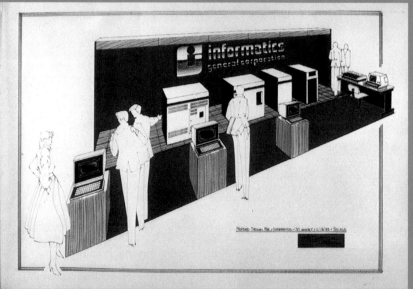

Exhibitor: Informatics General Corporation
Designer: Cindie Squilla
Producer: Giltspur Exhibits/Pittsburgh,
               Pittsburgh, Pennsylvania

By removing the center sections of the backwall and the
natural oak parquet floor, this 30 ft. display can be used
in a 20 ft. figuration. The panels and the logo are
attached with velcro so they can easily be moved to any
location on the backwall.

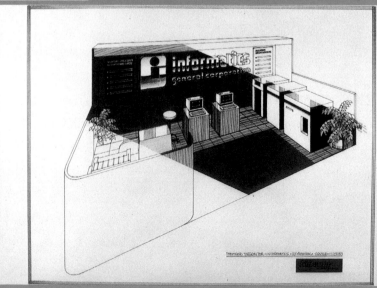

Exhibitor: Lanier Business Products
Designer: Sugar Creek Studios, Atlanta, Georgia
Producer: Sugar Creek Studios, Atlanta, Georgia

The central structure has a raised stage for demonstrations, while behind it is a theater with a multi-image presentation. There are ten modular units with flush light boxes, standing behind equipment pedestals for demonstration.

Exhibitor: AT&T Information Services
Designer: Alan Sitzer Associates
Producer: Alan Sitzer Associates/Industrial
Displays Inc., New York, New York

The exhibit is made up of modular interchangeable panels, 46×27 in. radiating from octagonal light columns. With the columns as hubs, the structure can be set up in a wide variety of arrangements. The graphics can easily be changed on site, without having to ship the entire assemblage to the shop.

Exhibitor: GTE
Designer: Structural Display, Inc.,
               Long Island, New York
Producer: Structural Display, Inc.,
               Long Island, New York

In order to permit uninterrupted hands-on
demonstrations, an island of quiet was established with
these units that offered the passer-by large, bright
transparencies. The heavy, curved frames helped build a
sense of unity.

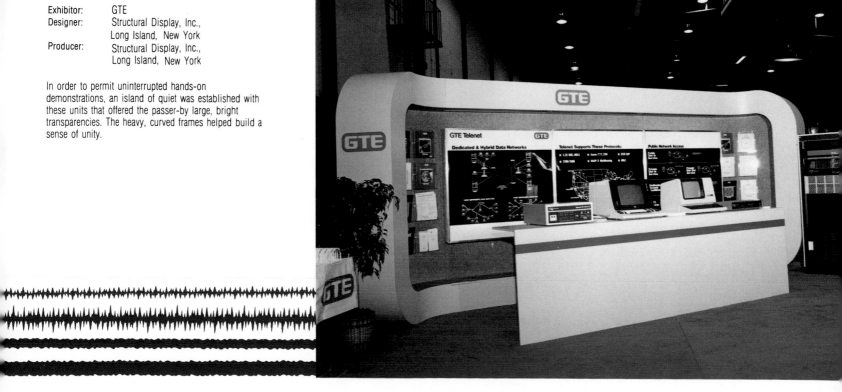

Exhibitor: Wirtschaftsverband Asbestzement
Designer: Walter Schmid-Herle
Producer: Messebau Laux und Söhne,
Heidelberg, West Germany

The open feeling created by the graceful curved walls, with their product photos and descriptions, invite the passer-by to step in. The curved headers unify the display, and the inner-illuminated globe emphasizes the slogan.

Exhibitor: Burroughs Corporation
Designer: Don Fee
Producer: Exhibit Works, Livonia, Michigan

To make a strong impression for the introduction of a new line of personal computers, the designer hung fabric banners from an overhead steel structure, which also served for clamp-on lighting. Exolite panels separate product areas and support changeable graphic inserts.

Exhibitor: Honeywell Inc.
Designer: Mark Mikulski
Producer: Haas Display Inc., Golden Valley, Minnesota

This large display, made of FOGA extruded aluminum components, includes many specific demonstration stands, as well as a small stage for presentations. The units can be reused in many smaller configurations.

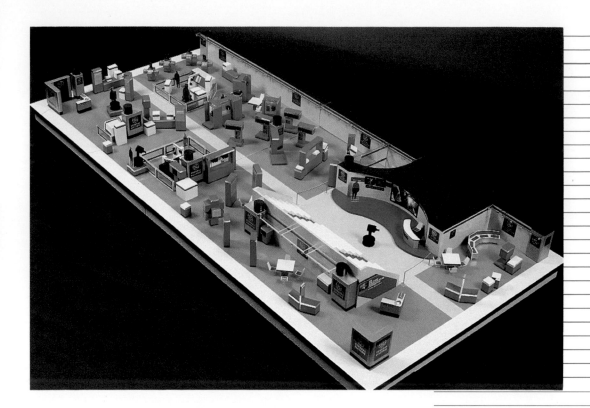

Exhibitor: General Electric Company
Designers: Tom Lemery, Gene Lindman
Producer: Cockade Ltd., London, England

A shell structure was built to incorporate a wide variety
of product developments with an overall corporate look.
The booth provides live demonstrations, conference areas,
graphics, video and product modules, plus equipment
from Europe integrated with GE components.

Exhibitor: Cilco Inc.
Designer: Miles Smith
Producer: Exhibitgroup Chicago, Chicago, Illinois

The modular concept worked very well here, giving four
workstations around each module.

Exhibitor: Lotus Development Corporation
Designer: Innovations Inc., Shrewsbury,
               Massachusetts
Producer: Innovations Inc., Shrewsbury,
               Massachusetts

In contrast to the busy, noisy, congested displays at most
computer shows, this simple exhibit is like an oasis.
Museum-like, it is cool, open, inviting, and spacious, yet
it contains ten computer workstations, an enclosed
theater, and a private conference room.

Exhibitor: Octanorm Vertriebs
Designer: Hans-Joachim Walter
Producer: Die Raumtechnik, Ostfildern,
               West Germany

Here the structure itself is the product, and the display was designed to show how use of a system does not hamper creativity.

Exhibitor: Berg & Company
Designer: ALGE Messebau, Swisttal-Heimerzheim,
               West Germany
Producer: ALGE, Messebau, Swisttal-Heimerzheim,
               West Germany

The exhibitor, a well-known manufacturer of clamping elements for milling machines, requested not only a perfect background for his products, but also two conference areas, a kitchen unit, and a performance and demonstration area. All this was to be based on the round shape of his products, with no angles, and the corporate colors of silver and black.

Exhibitor: United Technologies/Carrier Air
               Conditioning
Designer: Chuck Mack
Producer: Mack Studios, Auburn, New York

The highlight of this exhibit was a live performance on a built-in stage. The ceiling that bridged the center of the booth not only held the show lighting, but it controlled the ambient light of the hall.

Exhibitor: General Signal Corporation
Designer: E. Jeffrey Medler
Producer: Hanna Design Rochester Inc.

Use of the Radius Portable Panel System allowed three diverse groups within the company to build a unified exhibit which tied each to the corporation, but permitting each to have its own individual presentation area.

Exhibitor: Allied Automotive
Designer: John Switzer
Producer: Omnicraft Inc., South Bend, Indiana

Since the product was small and not especially glamorous, the eye-catching centerpiece of this display consisted of four cars, hoods open, displaying the parts in their normal environment. Display units around the center called attention to individual items.

Exhibitor: Dunlop Tire and Rubber
Designer: David Brace
Producer: David Brace Displays Inc., Alden, New York

For a booth intended to be used by two divisions of the exhibitor, as well as by corporate, an inflatable replica of the LeMans Dunlop pedestrian bridge, standing 20 ft. high, was used as a centerpiece, with product and panels being changed to suit the sponsor and the occasion. The grid ceiling helped unify and pull the entire booth, approximately 40 × 60 ft. together.

Exhibitor: Freightliner Trucks
Designer: Rod Schenken
Producer: Giltspur Exhibits/Los Angeles,
Los Angeles, California

A replica of an off-ramp proved to be an attractive
eye-catcher. The trucks, all painted to match the exhibit,
are actual models.

Exhibitor: Goodman Equipment
Designer: United Longchamp International,
Chicago, Illinois
Producer: United Longchamp International,
Chicago, Illinois

The truss ceiling was supported on open columns that
kept the open feeling of the space, and left more room
for equipment. Since the truss material can be dismantled
and re-used, the exhibitor was able to rent it for just one
year, at a considerable savings.

Exhibitor: Lifetime
Designer: Robert Blattner Design & Associates, Inc.
Producer: Structural Displays, Inc.,
              Long Island City, New York

Four audio-visual modules form the heart of this exhibit,
and are supported by other units, some of which carry
transparencies or TV monitors. Two conference rooms are
enclosed with plexiglass walls, and semi-private meeting
areas use modular couches. This exhibit has been utilized
in spaces ranging from 20 × 20 ft. up to 60 × 60 ft.

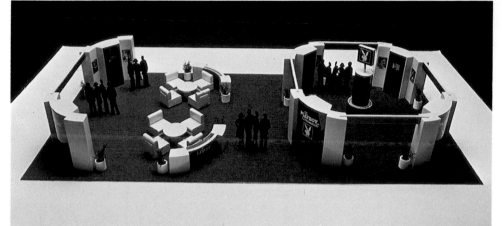

Exhibitor: Rainbow Programming Services
Designer: Robert Blattner Design & Associates, Inc.
Producer: Structural Displays, Inc.,
Long Island City, New York

With a product roster that included numerous items, which were constantly changing, this exhibitor needed an extremely flexible display. This design permits the easy replacement of backlit logos and transparencies, and even complete panels, yet maintains its sophisticated image.

TELEFUNKEN

Exhibitor:	Telefunken
Designer:	Expotechnik, Taunusstein, West Germany
Producer:	Expotechnik, Taunusstein, West Germany

This massive structure contained many working monitors and demonstration areas. The ceiling over the wall of monitors served not only to protect the screens from ambient light, but also as the support for the upper-deck area.

Exhibitor: Hitachi Sales
Designer: Karl Strobl
Producer: AMS, Vienna, Austria

The canopy and superstructure play a double role. The prominent place given to the exhibitor's logo makes sure it will be visible from much of the floor, and it also helps to control the ambient light that might affect the numerous video screens.

Exhibitor: Westinghouse
Designer: Don Graeb
Producer: Creative Productions, Pittsburgh, Pennsylvania

Designed for a public show, this exhibit featured a spectacular chandelier, 20 ft. in diameter, as well as trademarks in neon tubing.

Exhibitor: Nikon Inc.
Designer: Structural Display, Inc.,
Long Island City, New York
Producer: Structural Display, Inc.,
Long Island City, New York

The square cases balanced on their corners attracted attention, while the repeated logos gave strong corporate identification. The glass cases served to display a large number of pieces, and gave lots of usable demonstration area.

Exhibitor: Agfa-Gevaert
Designer: Karl Strobl
Producer: AMS, Vienna, Austria

The towers, placed along the perimeter of this island display, serve to call attention to the familiar name of this exhibitor.

Exhibitor: Anderson Corporation
Designer: Harvey Chandler
Producer: Haas Display Inc., Golden Valley,
                Minnesota

The perimeter of this 40×60 ft. exhibit was cantilevered
18 in. off the floor, to give the structure a floating
appearance. The elements could be rearranged for an
entirely new look, as seen in the smaller photo.

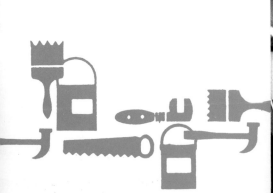

Exhibitor: Magicolor
Designer: Omnicom, Ltd., Elk Grove, Illinois
Producer: Omnicom, Ltd., Elk Grove, Illinois

Simulated paint buckets, pillars of color, and undulating
stripes made an exhibit that attracted the right people for
serious discussion.

Exhibitor: Adams Werbung GmbH + Company,
Göttingen, West Germany
Designer: Adams Werbung GmbH + Company,
Göttingen, West Germany
Producer: Adams Werbung GmbH + Company,
Göttingen, West Germany

When a display designer/builder, who also makes store fixtures, wanted to exhibit his fixtures at a trade show, he naturally did his own work. Hollow boxes were used to differentiate the product lines, and gave the needed wall space for mounting. Floor lights in color added interest to the whole.

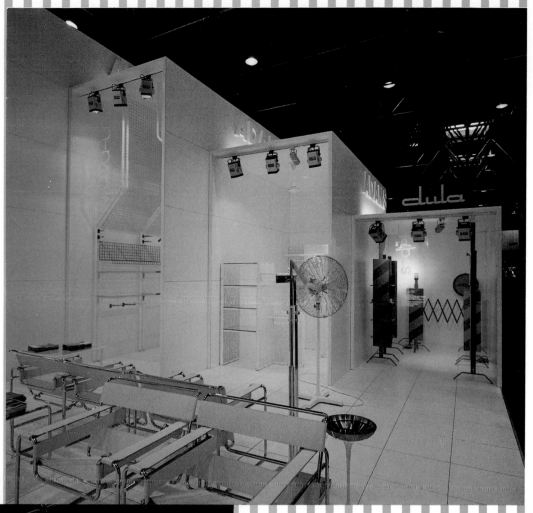

Exhibitor: National Gypsum Company
Designers: J. Marc Waller, Stephen LaBar
Producer: Hadley Exhibits, Buffalo, New York

A large overhead structure serves to unify seven different product divisions. Modular wall systems carry graphics and form backgrounds for product demonstration areas. To back up the theme of "Where Will Our Children Live," the designers specified helium-filled balloons, rotating overhead images of children, and children's mannequins at the base of the high central tower. The overhead structure and the wall system were planned for re-use the following year.

Chapter **5**

Giant Exhibits

Greater than 4,000 square feet/
371 square meters

Impressive, exotic, mammoth. These are just a few qualities of the spectacular exhibits contained in this chapter. They don't require elaborate graphics to catch the eye of passersby. Their sheer size—over 4,000 square feet/371 square meters—and prime location within most exhibit halls is enough to command the attention of prospective customers.

Perhaps the most effective super-exhibits are those that make a customer's visit memorable. A few exhibits in this collection used live entertainment, others impressive 50-seat theaters, and one group of seafood distributors made a big splash with a tank of fresh fish on ice. You'll also find massive displays of large equipment, spiral staircases, 27-foot high inflatable logos, and even one promenade deck.

Though the super exhibit is expansive enough to accommodate impressive architectural features, the designer must coordinate the various "zones" into a unified presentation. Consider, for example, the challenge in satisfying the marketing goals of 72 different companies within one exhibit.

The space must be differentiated for each company yet be part of a common visual theme and structural flow.

The same problem exists for the exhibit that showcases multiple product lines. The examples in this chapter illustrate the ways designers solved this problem. Designers of a multi-division exhibit for General Electric used a stripe to visually tie together various sections. For ITT Office Systems, the solution was in the structure of the exhibit itself, designers simulated an office building to demonstrate the ways in which various office automation systems work together. A theater in the center of the exhibit connected the individual offices.

Before tackling one of these projects, get out your yearly calendar because the super exhibit requires extraordinary lead time. Weeks, and then quickly months, will be consumed in planning these monstrosities. Several planning meetings with the client are necessary before the design process begins.

The designer will likely have to prepare a formal presentation and a three-dimensional model. There may be many layers of management to penetrate before getting approval for any one design strategy. The complex sketches will require frequent one-on-one consultations with the exhibit producer. The amount of materials needed to build such a colossus may exceed in-house inventory, especially if unusual materials are specified. Remember, too, that it takes longer to assemble the many sections of the super exhibit, and longer to package them for shipping. The large number of containers may require special shipping arrangements. Finally, at the exhibit site, plan extra time—and money—for on-site labor to construct the exhibit.

Exhibitor:	Ingrid
Designer:	Omnicom Ltd., Elk Grove, Illinois
Producer:	Omnicom Ltd., Elk Grove, Illinois

The strong colors of the plastic products are accentuated by the white of the pillars, the display walls, and the floor. The colors are repeated in the header that runs around the entire exhibit, holding it together visually.

Exhibitor:	Allied Chemical/Anso Fibers
Designer:	Omnicom Ltd., Elk Grove, Illinois
Producer:	Omnicom Ltd., Elk Grove, Illinois

The client's product is used, not only for the large decorative mural, but to cover pedestals as well.

Exhibitor: Batesville Casket Company
Designer: Barry M. Hatter
Producer: Alley Shop Inc., Cincinnati, Ohio

By concentrating the office/sales conference/theater in the center of the exhibit, the space for product display is maximized. Smoked plexiglass partitions, around the perimeter, serve as backgrounds for theme displays, as well as helping to direct traffic, without obstructing the view from the aisles. All copy is of vinyl letters.

Exhibitor: Krupp Industrietechnik
Designer: Fairconsult, Köln,
                West Germany

The second floor of this large exhibit area is reached by
a central spiral staircase. The cylindrical supports of the
deck allow plenty of space, not only on the periphery, but
also under the flooring, for display of heavy machinery.

Exhibitor: Wella AG
Designer: mmd Werbung u Design, München,
              West Germany
Producer: mmd Werbung u Design, München,
              West Germany

The prominent header, approximately 1,076 sq. ft. made
this booth easy to find, and also helped identify a central
demonstration area. Scattered throughout the booth were
locations where demos could be given to small groups.

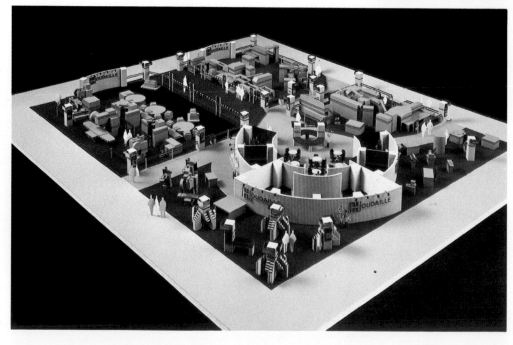

Exhibitor: Houdaille
Designer: Dave Klein
Producer: Creative Productions,
              Pittsburgh, Pennsylvania

Careful space planning was required to include several
demos of large equipment and a substantial area for
conference rooms and for storage.

Exhibitor: Chaussures de France
Designer: Pinkau-Messebau, Monheim,
               West Germany

The specially designed display stands were mirrored in
overhead structures. Meroform elements were used
throughout. Twenty separate companies exhibited in this
space of 8,611 sq. ft.

Exhibitor: U. S. Department of Commerce
Designer: Delta GmbH, Köln, West Germany
Producer: Delta GmbH, Köln, West Germany

In spite of the fact that there were 72 separate exhibitors,
each had three sides open, with one on the outside aisle.
The center spot was taken by a stage made of 2.5m
shipping crates, whose doors opened to present a fashion
show.

Exhibitor: General Electric/Hotpoint
Designers: Roy Romine, Jim Sackenheim,
              E Earl Heintzelman
Producer: Exhibitorgroup Cincinnati,
              Cincinnati, Ohio

Two facing islands, 40×115 ft. and 36×115 ft. were tied
together by the carpeting and similar structural elements.
The highest segment rises to 32 ft.

Exhibitor: Yamaha Division, West Germany
Designer: Pinkau-Messbau, Monheim,
West Germany

A display at a public show for motorcycles must satisfy the need of the visitors to feel and touch, as well as to see, the motorcycles, and the need of the manufacturer for exposure. Each of the categories of bikes was given a display center, like the one for rough terrain bikes shown here. A separate section of the display was reserved for the trade, where dealers could sit at functional booths in an area that could not be seen from outside, and have refreshments while they talked with company people.

Exhibitor: Yamaha Motor Corporation
Designer: Bobbi Vandiver
Producers: Exhibit Crafts Inc., Compton CA & LPI, Los Angeles, California

At this private show to introduce the 1985 product line, an opening feeling was desired so that some products would not be isolated. This was achieved by using overhead banners for product identification from any place in the room, while Scanamural panels provided action environments for each product line. The panels standing independently, will be used throughout the y for local and region shows throughout the country, with individual panels to meet the emphasis of the show.

Exhibitor: Atari Inc.
Designer: Steinheilber, Deutsch & Gard Inc.
Producer: Exhibitgroup San Francisco,
San Francisco, California

These photos were taken at three different set-ups of the same exhibit. The large inflatable replica of the logo was 27 ft. high and 24 ft. across, and is claimed to be the first application of an inflatable at a trade show. The two-level booth uses a standard Republic Steel industrial mezzanine system. The large deck permits major display and storage areas on the floor level, and as many as 23 office spaces above.

Exhibitor: Hitachi Seiki
Designer: United Longchamp International,
Chicago, Illinois
Producer: United Longchamp International,
Chicago, Illinois

Working within a strict height limitation of 8 ft., the designer used the truss system to create a central promenade. The truss elements were also used to unify the open space and to serve as a support for lights.

Exhibitor: Toshiba
Designer: Jörn G. Behrens
Producer: Display International, Würselen,
West Germany

An exciting wall of nearly 100 monitors is the eye-catcher in this large display, packed with multiple hands-on demonstration areas. The individual units are on movable mounts, making them easily accessible.

Exhibitor: ITT
Designer: Pico Art Pte., Ltd., Singapore
Producer: Pico Art Pte., Ltd., Singapore

To demonstrate a total office communications system, this open-concept display resembled an office, with a working system, giving a true-to-life representation of a modern office situation. A small theater was incorporated at the rear of the booth for private audio-visual presentations.

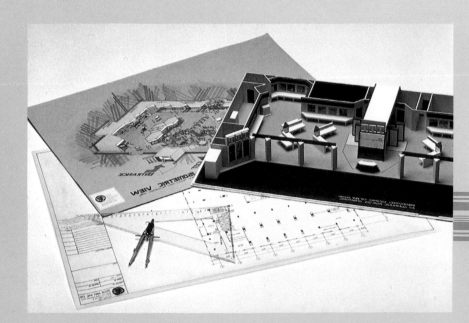

Exhibitor: Ford, Lincoln/Mercury
Designer: Dave Klein
Producer: Creative Productions,
                 Pittsburgh, Pennsylvania

The modular design reflects the sophistication of contemporary styling in presenting automotive parts and services to the aftermarket.

Exhibitor: Enesco Imports
Designer: Omnicom Ltd., Elk Grove, Illinois
Producer: Omnicom Ltd., Elk Grove, Illinois

In contrast to the crowded displays at most gift shows, this stands out in its seclusion, permitting buyers to examine merchandise without confusion. Each line of giftware is given its own space, almost like a boutique.

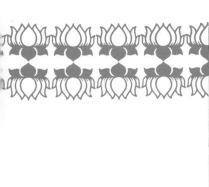

Chapter **6**

Demonstration Exhibits

*Demonstrations, theaters,
conference rooms*

Every exhibitor is familiar with the anticipation that builds, climaxing the instant before the doors to the exhibit hall first open. As the crowd surges through the entrance, eventually dispersing into the far corners of the exhibition hall, the exhibits begin to do their work. First they attract clusters of curious visitors, and then, hopefully lure prospective buyers into one-on-one discussions with sales personnel.

It's in these one-on-one discussions that the most important business is conducted. Where space permits, the designer must provide the appropriate setting for these meetings; secluded nooks or even fully private conference areas. The designer may also be called on to provide special spaces for demonstrations, live performances, and audio-visual presentations.

Despite the important role they play in facilitating the exhibitor's marketing objectives, these special areas shouldn't overpower other parts of the exhibit. Some visitors will want to make full use of these areas—watching demonstrations, viewing audio-visual presentations, and interacting with sales personnel. Others may simply want a quick introduction to the exhibitor's products. For this audience, the designer must accord equal emphasis to display panels which can be read quickly and to proper placement of sales literature.

A special area—a theater, demonstration area or stage for live performances—is sure to attract a large crowd, and so is often considered the centerpiece of an exhibit. For this reason, many designers place the special area in the center of the space, although, as you'll see in a few designs contained in this chapter, it can be equally effective to locate it away from the main flow of traffic. Conference areas are almost always segregated to ensure maximum privacy for one-on-one discussions. This can be achieved by placing them on a second level, or constructing a series of enclosed rooms to one side of the exhibit.

Whichever path is taken, it must be easy for visitors to enter and exit the special area. Time is valuable to trade show attendees. They may be reluctant to enter an enclosed space, particularly if they feel it will be difficult to leave during the presentation. One other consideration: Trade show sponsors often require that special presentations not interfere with neighboring exhibits or traffic flow in the aisles.

Despite these limitations, the illustrations in this chapter show the many clever ways designers have found to stage presentations for their clients.

Exhibitor: Westinghouse Groups W
Designer: Krent/Paffett Associates
Producer: Integral Productions, Staten Island,
             New York

Part of a major exhibit promoting cable television, this
group of full-size plaster lifecasts of sports fans is placed
on a bleacher section and dramatically lit. The television
sets show alternately the heads of the fans and
promotional sports programs.

Exhibitor:	Fisher-Price Toys
Designers:	Jack Snyder, Linda Scarfia, and Brion Charters
Producer:	Design for Industry Inc., Buffalo, New York

To introduce a new construction toy, Fisher-Price wanted an exhibit that could be set up in shopping center malls which would permit children (and perhaps adults) to play with the toy. The entire display structure was made of enlarged replicas of CONSTRUX. It travels in its own tractor trailer.

Exhibitor: GMC Truck & Coach Operations
Designers: Ron Ferguson, Dee Shuck
Producer: Exhibitgroup Chicago, Chicago, Illinois

Designed primarily for public shows, the units can be
arranged to fit varying spaces, and can include a
performance stage when needed.

Exhibitor: Black & Decker
Designer: Martin Spicuzza
Producer: Cyclonics Inc., Medina, Ohio

The highlight of this exhibit was a demonstration unit, an actual car cut in half to show automotive parts, backed up with application photography throughout.

Exhibitor: Campbell Sales
Designer: Emil Al Mellow II
Producer: Display Arts Studios Inc.,
New Castle, Delaware

One end of this exhibit was used for demonstration and sampling, while the other was devoted to an isolated nook for more private conversations. Each half of this display could be used as an independent entity.

Exhibitor: Miller Brewing Company
Designer: Rick Lewis
Producer: Exhibitgroup Chicago, Chicago, Illinois

Included in the space are a service bar area for sampling of the product, a performance area with an overhead mirror for a trick-shot pool expert, and space to conduct sales discussions with retailers.

Exhibitor: Paper Converting Machine Company
Designer: The Derse Company, Milwaukee,
             Wisconsin
Producer: The Derse Company, Milwaukee,
             Wisconsin

This simple unit conceals two private rooms, used for
conferences and for storage behind the backwalls.
Attention is focused on the machine in the center. The
backwall can be used by itself for a 40 ft. in-line display.

Exhibitor: NCR
Designer: Rod Schenken
Producer: Giltspur Exhibits/Los Angeles,
             Los Angeles, California

For a demonstration of a computer at work, a replica,
enlarged 700 times was built. Rear projection was used
to put graphics on the monitor, while the live
demonstrator worked out front.

Exhibitor: Interad
Designer: Convention Exhibits Inc.
Producer: Convention Exhibits Inc.

Modular units provide semi-isolated and completely closed conference/demonstration areas.

Exhibitor: Sperry
Designer: Dave Klein
Producer: Creative Productions,
Pittsburgh, Pennsylvania

A central stage and demonstration area left lots of room for people in this 40×40 ft. booth. Smaller units around the periphery were used for personal contact.

Exhibitor: Priam
Designer: David Jakel
Producer: Formetrics Inc., San Jose, California

The company's classical name was supported, both physically and in image, with classical columns, around which conference and demonstration areas were developed.

Exhibitor: McCloskey Varnish
Designer: C. Gruszka
Producer: Sparks Exhibits, Pennsauken, New Jersey

By incorporating the client's paint and varnish products into the material scheme of the booth, this design efficiently and attractively solved a problem of product display in a limited space. The conference room is a separate unit which can be removed when space is limited.

Exhibitor: Nicolet/Zeta
Designer: Gordon Murray
Producer: A. D. Gordon Company, Oakland, California

The output of the equipment in the display was used as part of its graphics attraction. In particular, the plotter produced topographical images of Mt. St. Helens, which had recently erupted. These attracted attention which transferred itself to the equipment.

Exhibitor: Sandoz Pharmaceuticals
Designer: Shlomo Almog
Producer: Holker & Barry, Inc.,
Brooklyn, New York

These semi-circular modules can be transformed from light boxes to rear-projection units, to learning carrels simply by inserting special housings and shelves that travel with the modules. This permits the exhibit to be altered from show to show without returning to the shop for refitting.

Exhibitor: Du Pont Company
Designers: Randy Childress, Dennis Van Sickle
Producer: Art Guild Inc., West Deptford, New Jersey

This island booth allowed for two kinds of demonstrations. One was wide open, easily reached by casual visitors, while the other was more secluded, although not shut off, where more serious visitors could see the equipment in operation, or even use it themselves.

Exhibitor: Steelcase Inc.
Designer: The Derse Company, Grand Rapids,
             Michigan
Producer: The Derse Company, Grand Rapids,
             Michigan

Central to this exhibit was a 20 ft. high cube tower,
attracting attention to an interactive computer display.
Other smaller demonstration areas were also included.

Exhibitor: Steelcase Inc.
Designer: The Derse Company, Grand Rapids,
             Michigan
Producer: The Derse Company, Grand Rapids,
             Michigan

Tubular steel columns controlled traffic in and out of the
theater area, where a demonstration was given. Low
panels and theatrical lighting simulated an open office
environment.

Exhibitor: Gould Inc., Defense Electronics Division
Designers: J. Marc Waller, Stephen LaBar

This demonstration diorama illustrates the uses of Gould's underwater sensing equipment. Ten different scenarios were staged with miniature ships and submarines.

Exhibitor: Du Pont Company
Designer: John Sereduke
Producer: Art Guild Inc., West Deptford, New Jersey

This demonstration unit shows the product, a solid plastic slab, in actual use in replicas of a kitchen and a wet bar.

Exhibitor: Uniroyal, Inc.
Designers: Don Fee, Steve Hough
Producer: Exhibit Works, Livonia, Michigan

The objective of this unit was to show how many stock
components the exhibitor supplies. The walk-around
exhibit featured a negative automobile shape, with the
various components floating on clear plexi supports.

Exhibitor: Gidding & Lewis
Designer: Exhibit Marketing Consultants
Producer: Hartwig Exhibitions, Milwaukee, Wisconsin

This full scale model of a 39-station robot drill head was accurately constructed of wood, and mounted in working position on the shell of a new automobile to demonstrate new technology.

Exhibitor: General Electric Company
Designers: Tom Lemery, Gene Lindman
Producers: Goodrich Displays, Albany, New York; Giltspur Exhibits/Rochester, Rochester, New York

Operating robots require a wide safety margin and thus detailed copy could not be placed on the backwall, since it would be too far away. Graphic panels were therefore placed on the rails, with large title panels on the backwalls, which were surmounted by 4 ft. high extensions to the 7 ft. 6 in. backwall, to increase visibility.

Exhibitor: American Motors
Designer: Stuart Stone
Producer: George P. Johnson Company, Warren, Michigan

These interesting demonstration platforms have rotating platforms which carry the cars and an interesting floral planter. The open sides permit large groups to watch and listen to the live narrator.

Exhibitor: Esprit
Designer: Steinhilber, Deutsch & Gard Inc.
Producer: Bluepeter Exhibits, San Francisco,
               California

This unusual structure has been used in a trade show,
but its more common use is in making sales
presentations in hotel rooms. In order to speed up the
process of buyers inspecting the line, the design can
accommodate two buyers at one time. The clothing is
pre-loaded on wire grid panels that run on overhead
trolley rails. These panels can be slid out either to the
right or the left for viewing. This enables two sets of
presenters and buyers to work simultaneously. Privacy is
achieved by closing Levolor blinds.

    The frame and open web trusses are made of thin wall
steel tubing, and are held together by large thumbscrews.
The trolley and tracks are standard Uniweb items. Two
unskilled people, usually the presentors, can set up this
unit in less than two hours, without using any tools.

Chapter 7

Multi-Level Exhibits

Double-deck Structures

If space is at a premium, the designer shouldn't neglect to look up—a second level can effectively double the floor space of an exhibit and provide other benefits, not the least of which is significant cost savings. Industry sources estimate that exhibitors save 30 percent in construction costs if they add a second level instead of expanding the exhibit horizontally. As a general rule, it costs no more per square foot to install a multi-level exhibit than a single-level one.

Clearly, the most popular use for a second level is to accommodate private conference areas. In this chapter, however, are several examples of other uses for this space. AT&T International, for example, created a multi-purpose upper deck which housed office space for exhibit administration, a theater, press office, conference rooms, lounge, restrooms, and a kitchen.

A second level needn't be this elaborate. The extra space can be used solely as a hospitality area in which to serve refreshments, or even meals, to visitors. It can also be used to display products too new to be shown to the general public.

There are as many clever uses for the outside of a second level structure as there are in the inside. Some exhibitors treat the second story as an advertising vehicle. The second floor structure of Protocol Computers' exhibit, featured in this Chapter, held a rear projection screen which displayed a continuous slide show to passersby. It also supported two moving message boards high enough for all to see.

Two-story exhibits aren't all blue sky, however. The structure has to be solid and safe; carefully engineered and constructed to bear the weight of equipment and people. Many exhibit show contracts specifically exempt the show sponsor and exhibit hall from responsibility for accidents occuring inside an exhibitor's display. The exhibitor faces potential legal liability if his second-floor structure is unsafe.

Designers may experience increasing demand for two-floor exhibits. Limitations of floor space in the most popular trade shows may force many exhibitors to "look up" for their future.

A second floor poses other challenges as well. Will a ceiling over the first floor make some areas seem claustrophobic? The designer must also muffle the flooring on the second level to minimize the amount of unwanted sound transmitted through the floor to the first level.

Exhibitor: ADAC Laboratories
Designers: M. Adkisson-Bicker, S. Nelson
Producer: Formetrics Inc., San Jose, California

The large cantilever of this design allows most of the floor to be used for demonstration area, while increasing the available area for conference rooms above. The support bases function as light boxes and storage areas. The two pods can be linked together with a bridge, or used separately.

Exhibitor: Eastman Kodak
Designer: Ron Ferguson
Producer: Exhibitgroup Chicago, Chicago, Illinois

Modular units, 4×5 ft. display radiograph transparencies, while the entire second floor is devoted to equipment and conference rooms.

Exhibitor: Motorola Semiconductor Products Inc.
Designer: Alex Klimov
Producer: Exhibitgroup Chicago, Chicago, Illinois

A small conference area is on the second level of the cylindrical information module.

Exhibitor: IBM Deutschland
Designer: Werner G. Dietrich

This large bi-level exhibit, with a relatively open ground
level, features exposed trusses which give a sense of
unity to the whole.

Exhibitor: Protocol Computers
Designer: Universal Exhibits, South El Monte, California
Producer: Universal Exhibits, South El Monte, California

The second floor of this exhibit served many purposes. In addition to a private selling area, in which refreshments could be served, the structure held a rear projection screen on each side on which a slide presentation was shown. It also held two moving message boards well above the traffic pattern. The workstations on the lower level were designed so that booth attendants could face the audience and direct them through the product description.

Exhibitor: Dana Corporation
Producer: Exhibit Works, Livonia, Michigan

Massive columns, each of which holds illuminated
product panels, supports a 20×20 ft. second-level
conference room.

Exhibitor: The Disston Company
Designer: Martin Spicuzza
Producer: Cyclonics Inc., Medina, Ohio

To achieve the maximum amount of floor space for
product display and demonstrations, a multi-level, open
structure was developed. Made of wood to reflect the
outdoor nature of the company's products, the exhibit
used live trees to add to the impact.

Exhibitor: Bucyrus Erie
Designer: The Derse Company, Milwaukee,
             Wisconsin
Producer: The Derse Company, Milwaukee,
             Wisconsin

The upper deck permits visitors to see the central piece
of machinery from a different angle. Scale models were
used to show products that were not featured.

Exhibitor: Walker
Designer: The Derse Company, Racine, Wisconsin
Producer: The Derse Company, Racine, Wisconsin

This is just one of the ways in which the elements of this
display can be put together. Conference rooms can be on
an upper or a lower level, and can be utilized in spaces
from 10 ft. in-line to the 20×80 ft. shown here.

Exhibitor: Nordicware
Designer: Darold Johnson
Producer: Haas Display Inc., Golden Valley,
Minnesota

In addition to the 24×37 ft. conference room on the upper level, this has a complete self-contained kitchen.

Exhibitor: Eternit Aktiengesellschaft
Designer: Walter Schmid-Herle
Producer: Messebau Horst und Günter Wiertula,
Berlin, West Germany

The massive tower, with its central panels, sets the pattern for the shapes used in this large exhibit. In addition to product demonstrations and semi-private conference areas on the ground level, there is an information center and a multi-medium theater. The upper level contains conference areas, as well as kitchen space.

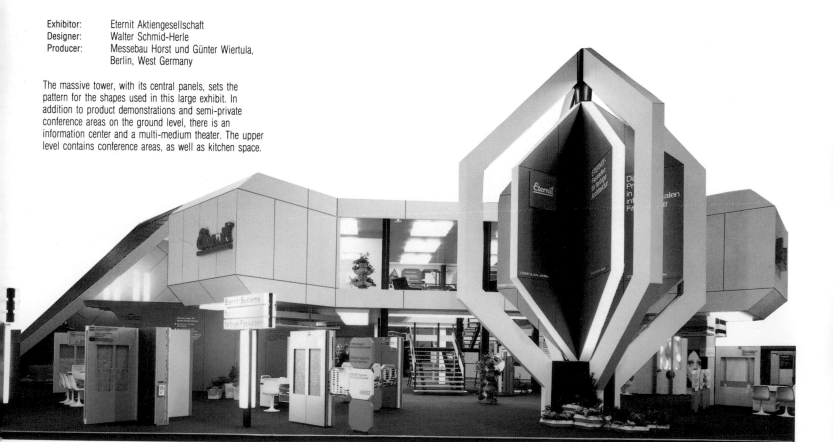

Exhibitor: Robbins & Myers
Designer: Martin Spicuzza
Producer: Cyclonics Inc., Medina, Ohio

This multi-leveled canopy provided opportunity to display a large number of ceiling fans without clutter, in an architectural setting that suggested the end use. A spiral staircase led to the upper level.

Exhibitor: Norelco/N. A. Philipps Lighting
Designer: Exhibit Graphics, Inc., Maspeth, New York
Producer: Exhibit Graphics, Inc., Maspeth, New York

The upper level, covering the entire booth area of 30×70 ft. is reached by a staircase that separates the spaces devoted to each of the two exhibiting divisions. It has six conference rooms and a lounge conference area. All units are modular, with concealed steel beams for support. Each of the two sections can be used separately.

Exhibitor: Rockwell Graphic Systems
Designer: Hans-Joachim Walter
Producer: Planbau, Essen, West Germany

Highlight of this large exhibit is the triple-chambered
visitors space on the upper level, called the shuttle
lounge by its designer.

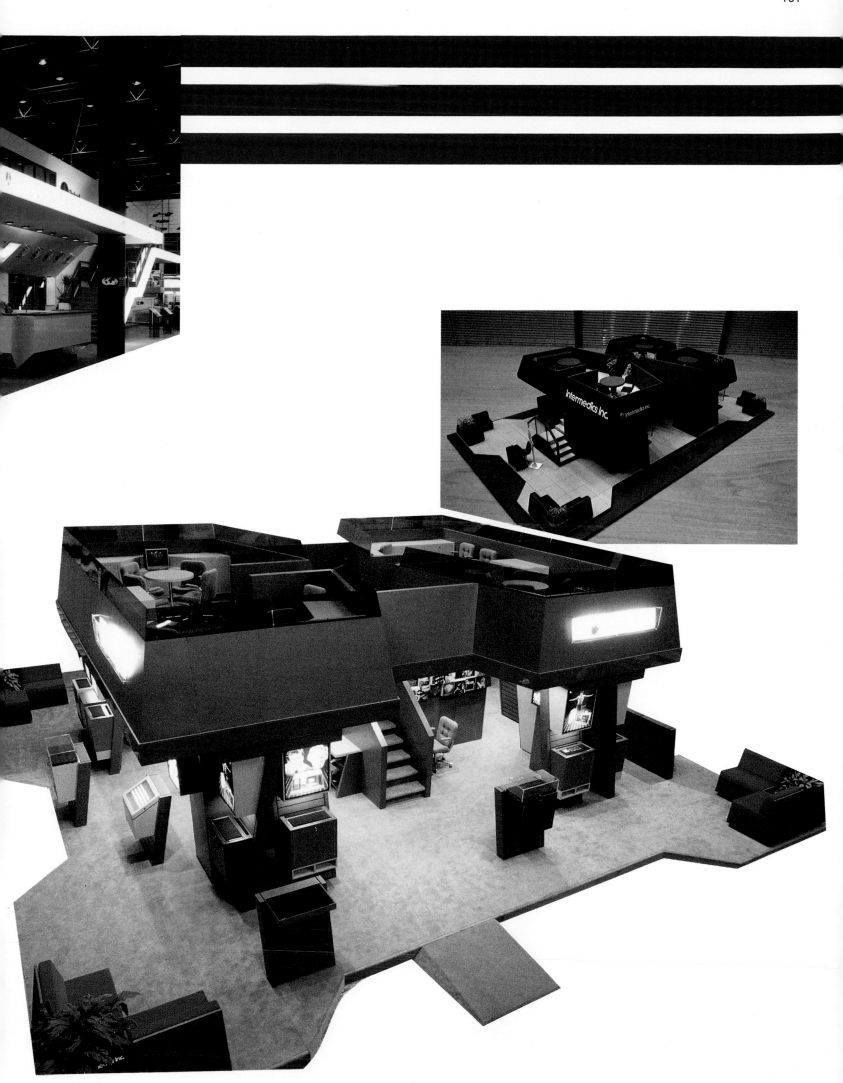

Exhibitor: TDK Electronics Corporation
Designer: Aaron Hirsch
Producer: Structural Display Inc., Long Island City,
             New York

This two story exhibit has its own air-conditioning
system, a built-in telephone system with a switchboard,
and a computer room.

Exhibitor: Taylor Instruments
Designers: Louis Siy, Thomas Finn
Producer: Ontario Design Inc., Rochester, New York

This entire, two-story structure, 130×30×18 ft., was
made from Click aluminum extrusions, and included a
product turntable, a 40-seat theater, and a customer
lounge on the upper level. The 12-projector slide show
presented an overview of product features. At this
conclusion, the screen rose, dramatically revealing the
product on the turntable.

Exhibitor: Intel
Designer: Rod Schenken
Producer: Giltsur Exhibits/Los Angeles,
             Los Angeles, California

This exhibit could be rearranged to fit spaces 20×30 ft.,
30×30 ft., or 40×40 ft., with all configurations allowing
for a second-story conference area.

Exhibitor: Standard Electrik Lorenz
Designer: Expotechnik, Taunusstein, West Germany
Producer: Expotechnik, Taunusstein, West Germany

Notice the open upper deck, on which visitors can have refreshments while they enjoy an overlook of the show floor.

Exhibitor: AT&T International
Designer: Plumb Design Group
Producer: Advertising Services Ltd.,
               Sheffield, England

The exhibit structure is of molded fiberglass components hung on a two-story steel frame. The central core is used for exhibit administration, and the space includes a theater, press office, conference rooms, lounge, restroom facilities, and a kitchen. Throughout the exhibit, the interactive video terminals describe worldwide activities, and video games of new technology engage the audience, adding a vital dimension of participation.

Chapter **8**

Dual Purpose Exhibits

The trade show, with its tough shoulder-to-shoulder competition, isn't the only setting for trade exhibits. Some are found far from the madding crowds of the exhibition hall, in building lobbies, corporate cafeterias, and auditoriums.

Designers may be asked to produce an exhibit that can be used both at trade shows and in other settings. Some of the examples in this chapter do this kind of double duty. The ways in which these dual-purpose displays have been employed is a tribute to the ingenuity of marketing and public relations people.

While the techniques of design and construction are constant, displays for trade shows and those for other settings are radically different. Their audiences are different. And, while the trade show booth gives the exhibitor's sales people a ready-made sales environment, exhibits mounted elsewhere are often unmanned. These differences must be reflected in design and construction.

Ordinarily, trade show attendees have been pre-qualified by the show's sponsor; they have a professional interest in the industry represented by the show. In other settings, exhibits often serve a broader audience which has little interest in the exhibit's theme and little prior knowledge of its content. A materials buyer attending a plastics convention needn't be sold on the importance of learning about a new plastics manufacturing process. Therefore, the exhibit showcasing it can be devoted to explaining the technology in great depth to a presumably knowledgeable viewer. By contrast, if the exhibit is to be viewed by the general public, wall panels depicting the process would have to be simplified and highlighted with eye-catching graphics designed to explain why passersby should take the time to study the exhibit. And, since the display won't be manned by technical or sales people, it had better tell the full story.

This places a heavy burden on the designer to ensure that audio-visual presentations are fully automated, and that the equipment specified for them is foolproof, absolutely safe to leave unattended, and mechanically reliable. Motion displays must be designed so there isn't the slightest possibility of a viewer being injured, with adequate guards to keep the inquisitive well away from

moving parts and electrical connections. The designer may rely more on printed materials. If free literature is provided, dispensers should be clearly labeled. People often hesitate to pick up brochures unless they are certain the material is free for the taking.

While it's certainly possible to adapt a trade show exhibit for use in other venues, the cost of properly converting it may be higher than simply building a new display from the ground up. Whichever approach is taken, the work on the following pages shows how it can be done effectively and with style.

Exhibitor: Diesel Construction Company
Designer: Gene Lindman
Producer: Gene Lindman Design, Hoosick Falls,
              New York

Rather than using graphic panels or photos in a very
tight space, screenprinting was done on vinyl wall fabric
and applied directly to the wall. The result is very durable
and, unlike photos, washable.

Exhibitor: American Express
Designer: Dick Portner
Producer: Outline, Waltham, Massachusetts

This public service exhibit was designed to be set up in
public locations, in support of the campaign for the
rehabilitation of the Statue of Liberty. Easy portability was
a prime requirement.

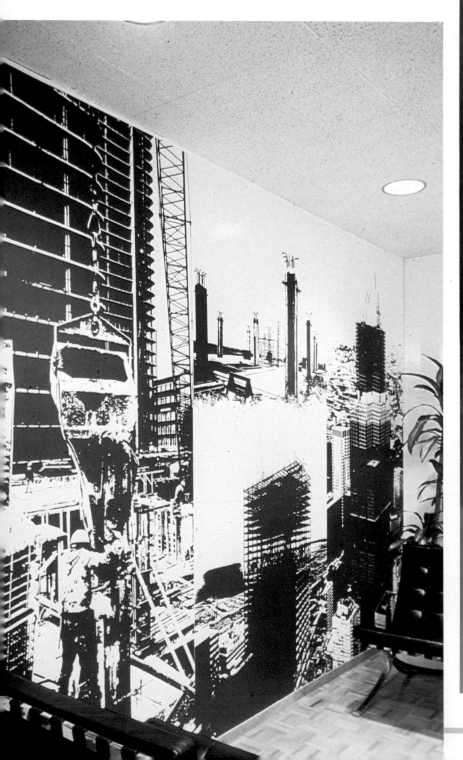

Exhibitor: Talman Savings & Loan Association
Designer: Gene Lindman
Producer: Gene Lindman Design, Hoosick Falls, New York

The unusual element here is that the high-contrast photos are black and white prints, wet mounted with the edges wrapped around a rigid sheet. They were then given a solid color dye wash. In this way large prints can be used, achieving custom colors at a cost well below screen printing.

Exhibitor: Boonton Molding Company
Designer: Robert Blattner Design & Associates Inc.
Producer: Structural Displays Inc.,
              Long Island City, New York

The challenge was to design, renovate, and install — in four weeks — a unique reception area & waiting room, combined with a corporate exhibit.

Exhibitor: Graphic Arts Technical Foundation
Designer: Monkey Bars
Producer: The Nimlok Group, Morton Grove,
              Illinois

Each of these panels is self standing, due to a return on each side, and they can thus be placed in a variety of configurations. Here they are used in a hallway as a welcoming sign to a meeting.

Exhibitor: Borg Warner
Designer: Paul McGean Jr.
Producer: Creative Productions, Pittsburgh,
                Pennsylvania

Striking graphics on this travelling, self-contained theater
called attention to itself, both on the highway or parked
for use. The van is often driven onto the floor to serve as
the audio-visual element of a trade show.

Exhibitor: Fa Conzen
Designer: Wolfgang Pinkau
Producer: Pinkau Messebau, Monheim,
West Germany

For a fashion show held in the inner court of an old building in Düsseldorf, open to the weather, a structure of Meroform was installed to hold a roof of transparent sheeting to protect people from the rain. This structure also served as a lighting scaffold.

Exhibitor: Trammell Crow Company
Designer: Jon Gunderson
Producer: Freeman Design/Display Company,
Dallas, Texas

This highly visible, free-standing kiosk is intended for use in various lobby locations to enhance the knowledge of the exhibitor's various marketing and development projects. Marble and brass were used to indicate the quality of the company.

Exhibitor: General Electric Co., Mobile
Communications Division
Designers: J. Marc Waller, Stephen LaBar
Producer: Berm Studios, Yeadon, Pennsylvania

This permanent product display area uses stainless steel and subtle grays to pick up the feeling of the division's trade show exhibits. The graphic panels and the product line titles are removable to allow for easy update. The independently-controlled fluorescent and incandescent lighting systems provide for distinctive moods in the room.

Exhibitor: Magnavox
Designer: Omnicom Ltd., Elk Grove, Illinois
Producer: Omnicom Ltd., Elk Grove, Illinois

In an unusual move, this exhibitor decided to have his exhibit at a major trade show removed from the main floor and installed in a separate space at the exhibition hall. This permitted the product to be shown in lifestyle vignettes in comfortable, uncrowded settings.

Exhibitor: Missouri State Highway Patrol
Designer: Pingel Displays, Inc., St. Louis, Missouri
Producer: Pingel Displays, Inc., St. Louis, Missouri

In a 10 ft. space, this exhibit includes a diorama of a rural railroad crossing with sequential color-coded lights to depict increasing danger, and an electronically-activated multiple choice game with an audio signal for the correct answer.

Exhibitor: DuPont Company
Designer: Dennis Van Sickle
Producer: Art Guild Inc., West Deptford, New Jersey

Designed as a corporate posture presentation, this exhibit is unified by a basic unit design, and demonstrates the wide variety of products and interests in which the exhibitor is involved.

Exhibitor: Colonial Williamsburg Foundation
Designer: Teddie Ryan
Producer: Beyond Exhibits Inc., Newport News,
Virginia

Meeting very rigid installation requirements, this unit
displayed authentic reproductions that were available for
purchase.

Exhibitor: Michigan Bell
Designer: Stuart Stone
Producer: George P. Johnson Company, Warren,
               Michigan

The interior design and the exhibit units are coordinated to express a high-tech communications quality throughout the entire complex. Some exhibits are hands-on, while others must be operated by company personnel. A comfortable presentation room is a major element in the center.

Exhibitor: Honeywell Inc.
Designer: Cy Schlosser
Producer: Haas Display Inc., Golden Valley,
             Minnesota

This backdrop for a special corporate meeting is made of
FOGA extruded aluminum framing system. Measuring
50 ft. wide and 22 ft. high, it is flanked by two rear-
projection screens, each 28 × 10 ft.

Exhibitor: Honeywell
Designer: Ron Ferguson
Producer: Exhibitgroup Chicago, Chicago, Illinois

A resource center for the building area, this installation
features a plexiglass mirror, with heroic silkscreened
graphics behind the receptionist's desk, and a circular
conference/meeting room, with a projection room behind
the seating area. All projection and lighting controls are
located in the podium unit.

A RESOURCE
CENTER
FOR THE
BUILDING
INDUSTRY

THE RESPONSIVE ENVIRONMENT THE RESPONSIVE ENVIRONMENT THE RESPONSIVE ENVIRONMENT

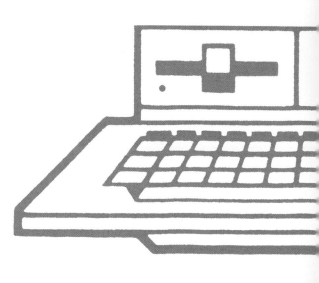

Exhibitor: Virginia Electric and Power Company
Designer: Teddie Ryan
Producers Beyond Exhibits Inc., Newport News,
Virginia, Exponents Inc., San Diego,
California

Six of these free-standing kiosks were created to help the exhibitor celebrate its 75th anniversary throughout the state. Each had enough flexibility to be adapted to difficult and varied space requirements.

IN ELECTRIC METERING.

OUR FUTURE... A COMMITMENT TO CONTINUING EXCELLENCE

Exhibitor: General Electric Company
Designers: Tom Lemery, Gene Lindman, Dennis Rackowski
Producer: Global Exhibition Services, Brooklyn, New York

The entrance lobby of the Meter Department is devoted to the story of over 100 years of product development. Artifacts and panels, some opaque and some rear-illuminated, are set in oak frames against a dark carpeted panel that seems to float from the wall, curving out both top and bottom. Lighting washes both the ceiling and floor, as well as illuminating the header from the rear.

Exhibitor: Exxon Office Systems
Designer: Dirk Haas
Producer: Giltspur Exhibits/Rochester, Rochester, New York

This special area, located in corporate headquarters, is intended to give important prospects a hands-on demonstration of new products and the integrated product line. An audio-visual and conference room is also included.

Chapter 9

Museum Exhibits

Not all exhibits are intended to sell products; some sell ideas. Educational and museum displays are among these types of displays. While there are similarities in design and construction techniques, educational exhibits are vastly different from commercial ones.

Trade show exhibits are, in essence, a stage and a theater for the exhibitor's sales force. Well-trained company representatives press home the points made by the exhibit. Most educational exhibits are unmanned, and must rely on graphic displays and machines to interact with the visitors. As these examples show, the only limitations on the designer's imagination are his own creativity and the project budget. For the Louisiana World's Fair, the U.S. Army Corps of Engineers brought a mammoth dredging barge out of retirement to house an equally mammoth exhibit explaining the Corps' work on the Mississippi River. An entrance was cut in the side of the barge. Inside, a 60-foot-long model of the river demonstrated how sediment collects along the banks and in the river's shipping channel. In another section, life-sized bronze statues of Corps workers depicted the construction of a lock and dam.

While the range of possibilities open to the designer of educational exhibits is broader, so is the audience. This affects everything from the intellectual level of the information presented to the viewing angle for graphics and the height of counters. The special needs of children and those with physical, visual or hearing handicaps must be met.

While the trade show exhibit will likely be taken apart, shipped, and reassembled in a number of locations, many educational exhibits are permanent. This frees the designer from the need for simplicity and portability, but imposes additional demands for structural soundness and durability.

Few trade show exhibits are larger than 4,000 square feet, but educational exhibits can be any size and placed in almost any kind of location. The river barge is one example. Another, illustrated in this chapter, was commissioned by the U.S. Department of Interior to tell the story of the Grand Coulee Dam. It occupies four major buildings and has auxiliary displays located around the entire sprawling dam site.

Another special consideration for museum designers is the display of rare or precious artifacts. Documents and books are extremely sensitive to temperature, humidity and sunlight. Often, artifacts must be enclosed in air tight, temperature controlled cases to prevent deterioration. For very valuable or rare pieces, security may be needed. Few trade exhibit designers have to worry about wiring display cases and panels with burglar alarms, yet most museum designers face this difficulty constantly.

While the items on display in the educational exhibit are, emphatically, not for sale, the ideas presented surely are. The designer must ensure that they are communicated as forcefully, clearly, and effectively as possible.

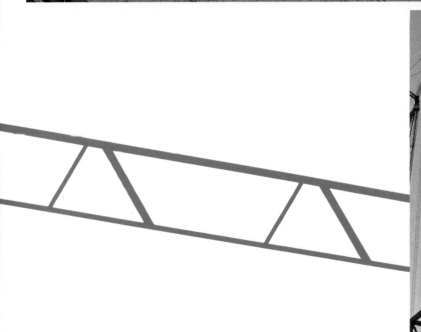

Exhibitor: U.S. Army Corps of Engineers
Designers: Peter Tasi, Ezra Wittner
Producer: Hargrove Inc., Lanham, Maryland

For the Louisiana World's Fair, the Corps of Engineers brought a Mississippi dredge out of retirement to house the story of the Corps and the river. In the center of a barge with an entrance ramp was a 60' abstract model of the Mississippi, made of acrylic tubing cut in lengths to suggest the relative depths of the river and colored to show sedimentation patterns. Another section shows the construction of a lock and dam, using life-size bronzed sculptures of Corps workers, with recordings of heavy equipment at work providing sound effects.

Exhibitor: U.S. Army Corps of Engineers
Designers: Peter Tasi, Ezra Wittner
Producer: Hargrove Inc., Lanham, Maryland

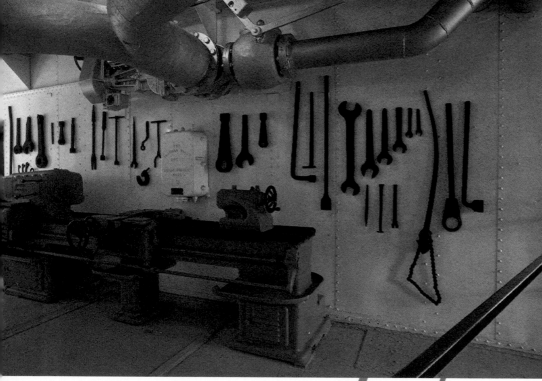

Exhibitor: U.S. Army Corps of Engineers
Designers: Peter Tasi, Ezra Wittner
Producer: Hargrove Inc., Lanham, Maryland

CHICAGO

Exhibitor: Museum of Science and Industry,
                    Chicago, Illinois
Designer: Herbst, LaZar, Rogers & Bell
Producer: Exhibitgroup Chicago, Chicago, Illinois

Entitled "Chicago — The I Will City," this exhibit was designed to capture the spirit of Chicago, in terms of history, present, and future. Following a foundation section, there were sections on science and industry, transportation, arts and culture, architecture, and the city. While complex techniques were used, including a visitor participation unit covering the history of the community, another permitting visitors to simulate guiding a plane to a landing, and a four-minute multi-medium presentation, many of the topics were covered with low technology exhibitry using purely graphic elements. The exhibit opened in 1977.

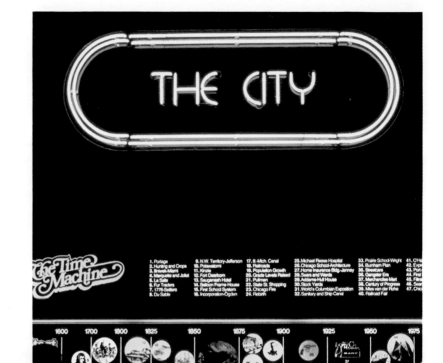

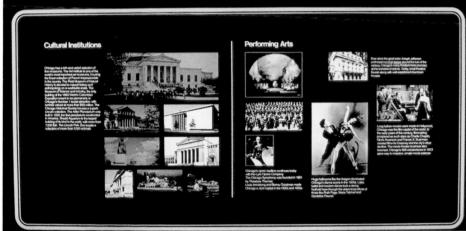

Exhibitor: International Museum of Photography at
                George Eastman House
Designer: Dirk Haas
Producer: Giltspur Exhibits/Rochester, Rochester,
                New York

This travelling exhibit, on the development of the
Japanese camera, was designed so that each case was its
own shipping case, with space for storing the cameras it
displayed and special locking and dust-tight doors.
Approximately 450 actual cameras were displayed.

Exhibitor: North Dakota Heritage Center
Designer: Krent/Paffett Associates
Producer: DisplayMasters, Minneapolis, Minnesota

Real artifacts are made more realistic by being displayed
in actual work conditions, with the aid of life-size plaster
figures.

Exhibitor: Iron Range Interpretive Center
Designer: Krent/Paffett Associates
Producer: General Exhibits Inc., Chicago, Illinois

A 1910 saloon was recreated and peopled with life-size
plaster casts. The card game being played is enhanced
by overhead projection, using the white table top as a
screen.

Exhibitor: Texas Twenty
Designer: Jane Corbus
Producer: Freeman Design/Display Company,
              Houston, Texas

The exhibit highlights 20 buildings that have left their
mark on Texas architecture.

Exhibitor: Academy of Natural Science
Designer: Norman Ikeda
Producer: Art Guild Inc., West Deptford, New Jersey

Cases specially designed to handle unusually shaped specimens feature this display of archeological discovery.

Exhibitor: Coyote Point Museum, San Mateo, California
Designer: Gordon Ashby
Producer: General Exhibits and Displays, Inc., Chicago, Illinois

This small museum concentrates on the ecology of the area in which it is located. The use of wood heightens the feeling of nature and the rural area. The pier structure allows visitors to look down on a stylized marsh area, whose strata cross-section is shown graphically on the left.

Designer: Ralph Lapham
Producer: Outline, Waltham, Massachusetts

Designed as a portable display, this unit is sturdy, clean in design, and easy to break down and erect.

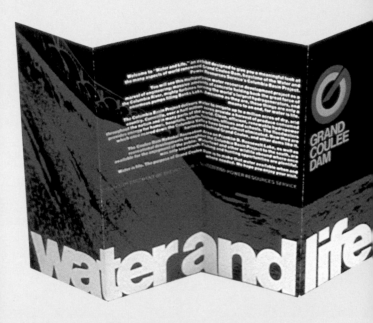

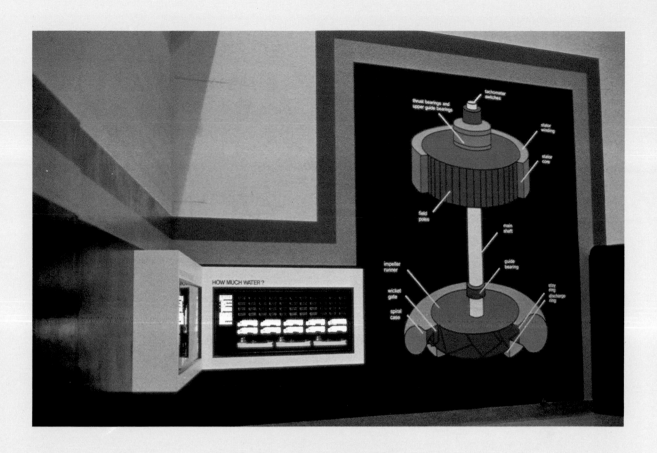

Exhibitor: U.S. Department of the Interior,
               Grand Coulee Dam
Designer: Herbst, LaZar, Rogers & Bell
Producer: Design & Production Inc., Alexandria,
               Virginia

This design project is geared to the casual visitor who stops at and visits the Dam, and until this exhibit was installed, found an enormously involved complex, far beyond his understanding. Through a major undertaking, the unguided visitor will now be able to fully comprehend all the workings and complexities of this facility on his own.

While specific exhibit works are scattered among four major buildings, the project also included graphics to be seen on a self-guided auto tour of the project, as well as observing some of the operating installations. At the Visitor Arrival Center, where most visits start, a giant theme mural, 10 × 65 ft., entitled "Water and Life," hangs over the reception desk. A 150-seat theater is used for an orientation film. Throughout the tour, visitors come across many graphic panels explaining what they are looking at, and there are also several "hands-on" opportunities for visitors, including two minicomputers.

Exhibitor: National Park Service
Designers: Bruce Collins, Daniel Quan
Producer: Exhibitgroup San Francisco,
              San Francisco, California

This exhibit employs open dioramas with static graphics
and interactive games to orient visitors to the Pt. Reyes
National Park. The exhibit is set up as a walkthrough of
the biotic communities found in the area.

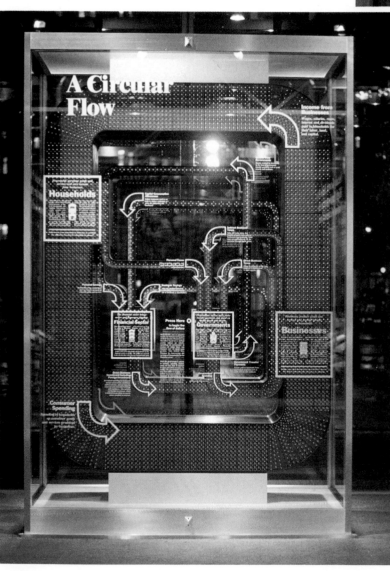

Exhibitor: Federal Reserve Bank of San Francisco
Designer: Howard Lathrop and Associates
Producer: General Exhibits and Displays Inc.,
               Chicago, Illinois

This public exhibit, designed to educate the general public on the complexity of the modern economic system, uses static, active, and interactive elements. The unit entitled "A Circular Flow," demonstrating the flow of money, contains approximately 17,000 micro-processor controlled LEDs. To activate the exhibits, the visitor touches a dummy push-button printed on the glass, thereby breaking an infrared beam.

Exhibitor: Honeywell
Designers: Don Graeb, George Coholich
Producer: Creative Productions, Pittsburgh, Pennsylvania

Installed in the Boston Museum of Science, this is a chronological presentation of information processing technology, from the beginning to a projection of future artificial intelligence. Animated areas with visitor interaction explains basic computer functions, while the focal area features the mainframe control center.

Exhibitor: National Air and Space Museum,
            Washington, D.C.
Designer: Herbst, LaZar, Rogers & Bell
Producer: Lynch Exhibits, Pennsauken, New Jersey

A permanent room in one of the museums of the
Smithsonian Institution, this exhibit covered the history of
rocketry, from early Chinese experimentation through
today's space flights and tomorrow's dreams.

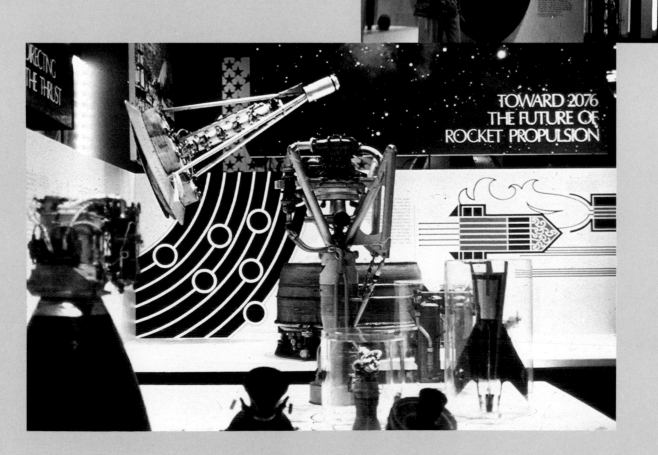

Exhibitor: City of Kiel
Designer: 3D-SIGN, Kiel, Federal Republic of
Germany
Producer: 3D-SIGN, Kiel, Federal Republic of
Germany

Mounted in 1972 in conjunction with the Olympics, this
exhibit's theme was "Man and the Sea."

Exhibitor: California State Capitol Museum
Designers: Bruce Collins, Daniel Quan
Producer: Loren Barr Exhibits, San Francisco,
               California

The exhibit uses actual pieces of the building and
restoration samples to tell the story of the reconstruction
of the State Capitol building.

Exhibitor: Bethune Museum
Designer: Jocelyn Voros
Producer: Joan Carol Associates,
               Suitland, Maryland

This museum exhibit, very lightweight and
portable, uses archival documents
and photographs.

Exhibitor: Pro-Rodeo Hall of Champions, Museum
of the American Cowboy
Designer: Design Dynamics, Denver, Colorado
Producer: Design Dynamics, Denver, Colorado

Bleachers and canvas are used to house a collection of
wild west artifacts and memorabilia.

Exhibitor: Cafe Kandahar and Ski Museum
Designer: Design Dynamics, Denver, Colorado
Producer: Design Dynamics, Denver, Colorado

Exhibits for this unusual combination museum/restaurant
fit into the warm ski lodge atmosphere.

Exhibitor: City of Kiel Press Department
Designer: Bernhard Schwichtenberg
Producer: 3D-SIGN, Kiel, Federal Republic of Germany

Showing the work of four photographers, this unusual approach to mounting a show was developed in 1969 for exhibition at the Copenhagen town hall.

Exhibitor: Wilson Certified Foods
Designers: Gene Lindman, John Drummond
Producer: Gene Lindman Design, Hoosick Falls, New York

In this installation, images from a local historical society were combined with current shots into a montage that visually tells of the company's growth and development. Note that the background is also done in panels, with frames to match the depth of the photos, but are covered in suede, giving the wall a soft look to set off the images.

Exhibitor: Pacific Science Center
Designer: Daniel Quan Design
Producer: Pacific Science Center, Seattle,
               Washington

This exhibit, entitled 'China: 7000 Years of Discovery,'
integrates static displays of arts and handicrafts with live
demonstration areas for craftsmen to perform their art.

Chapter 10

Systems and Concepts in Exhibit Design

Many of the exhibits illustrated in this book are unique, one-of-a-kind constructions. Yet not all were custom designed. Pressures to reduce construction and shipping costs have inspired designers to use stock, pre-fabricated materials. At the same time, suppliers have developed a number of advanced display systems and materials. It may be impossible to tell an exhibit built up of stock parts from one constructed from scratch. But, because the stock parts are manufactured in quantity, they may offer significant construction savings to the exhibitor.

Some of these exhibit systems require very little labor to set up, and few or no tools, producing further savings.

In addition, large exhibit houses may rent stock materials to exhibitors, drastically lowering the cost of the materials that make up a display. European exhibitors have made use of rented displays for years, and the practice is now spreading in the United States.

Not all exhibit systems are available on the open market. To simplify design and construction of trade exhibits, and to reduce costs, 3M designed its own exhibit system. Used by all of its divisions, the system consists of a limited number of components, all of identical construction and fully interchangeable.

General Electric, faced with the difficulties of combining exhibits for its many divisions into a coherent mass display for overseas trade shows, developed a striking series of modules that included a television production studio with bleachers for 150 people and a fully operational manufacturing cell manned by five robots.

Some of the systems illustrated here, such as those used by 3M and GE, are a far cry from early exhibit-in-a-suitcase models. Fortunately, development of systems that make up into large, even multi-level exhibits has been matched by refinements in the ultra-lightweight, ultra-portable systems. For some exhibitors, this exhibit-in-a-suitcase is necessary if they are to participate in trade shows at all.

Exhibitor:	Norlin Music
Designer:	Omnicom Ltd., Elk Grove, Illinois
Producer:	Omnicom Ltd., Elk Grove, Illinois

For an exhibition in Germany, the exhibitor needed soundproof rooms, and theater and product demonstration areas.

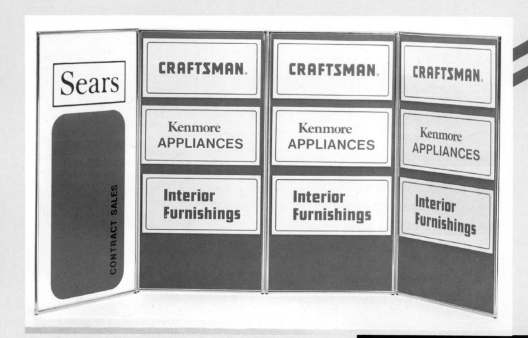

Producer: Technical Exhibits, Chicago, Illinois

Based on the Tech-Exhibit system, each of these displays is light enough to pack in cases that can be shipped by air as luggage. No tools are needed.

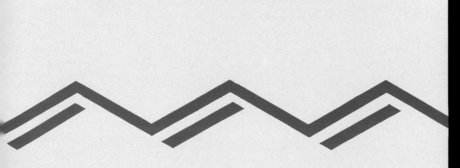

Exhibitor: Elgin
Designer: Cindie Squilla
Producer: Giltspur Exhibits/Pittsburgh,
               Pittsburgh, Pennsylvania

Each unit in this exhibit is a separate standing display case, spot-lit from above and with storage underneath. These units can be set up in almost any configuration.

218

Exhibitor: Bell Atlantic
Designer: Dave Harbaugh
Producer: Giltspur Exhibits/Pittsburgh,
Pittsburgh, Pennsylvania

Each of these modules provides a working demonstration
of high-tech electronic equipment, along with graphic
displays.

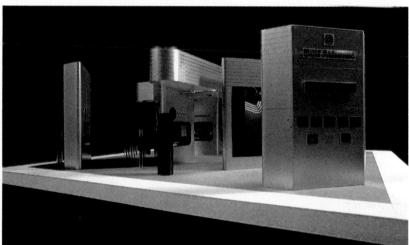

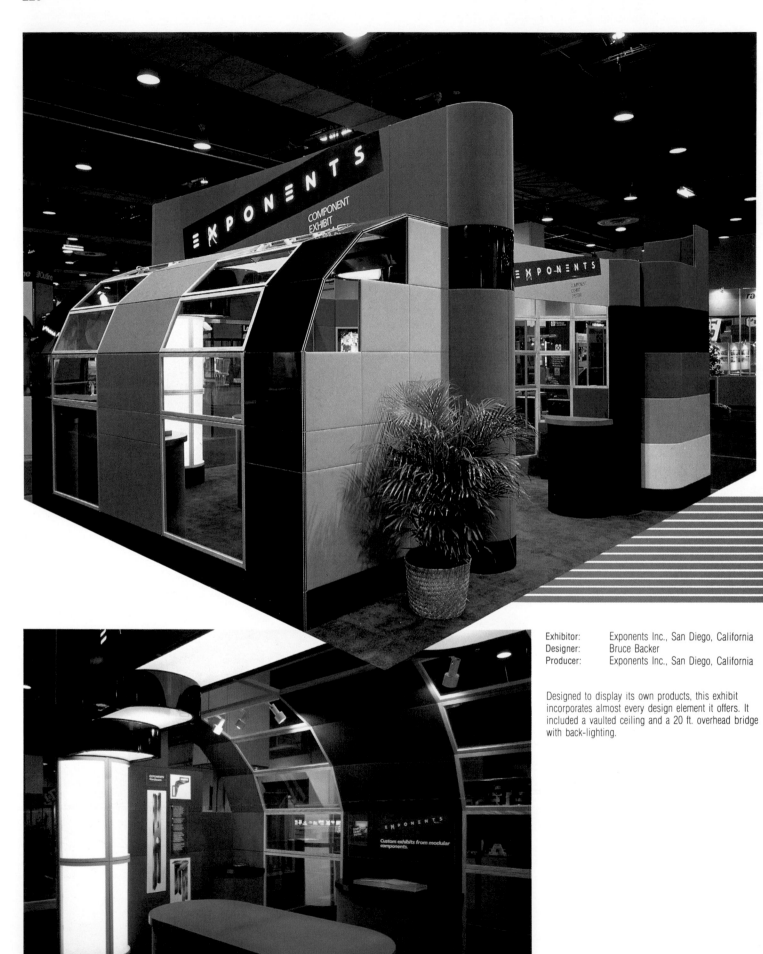

Exhibitor: Exponents Inc., San Diego, California
Designer: Bruce Backer
Producer: Exponents Inc., San Diego, California

Designed to display its own products, this exhibit incorporates almost every design element it offers. It included a vaulted ceiling and a 20 ft. overhead bridge with back-lighting.

Exhibitor: Microswitch
Designer: Convention Exhibits, Inc., Chicago, Illinois
Producer: Convention Exhibits, Inc., Chicago, Illinois

These modular units, each 3 ft. 3 in., come complete with overhead lights and easily attached headers. Changeable copy panels can stretch across one, two, or three modules.

Exhibitor: General Electric Company
Designer: Tom Lemery
Producers: Giltspur Exhibits/Rochester, Rochester, New York; Goodrich Displays, Albany, New York

A standard modular frame system (7 ft. 6 in. × 18 in., 24 in. or 37 in.) incorporated Velcro skins, electrical services, one-, two-, or three-way hinges. It could also be erected as a 2-level structure.

Exhibitor: National Exhibition
Designer: 3D/International
Producer: Pico Art Pte., Ltd., Singapore

Covering an area of 215,285 sq. ft. in three exhibition halls, plus 150,700 sq. ft. of open area, the National Exhibition celebrated Singapore's 25 years of nation-building. As can be seen from the pictures, a wide variety of techniques were used to tell a varied story.

Exhibitor: Miller Printing
Designers: Richard Koplar, Dorothy Clark
Producer: Giltspur Exhibits/Pittsburgh,
          Pittsburgh, Pennsylvania

To achieve a second-story structure within a 14 ft. height limitation, the deck was set on a 228 sq. ft. storage area. Overhead track lighting illuminates working printing equipment on demonstration. For smaller spaces, the conference area can stand alone.

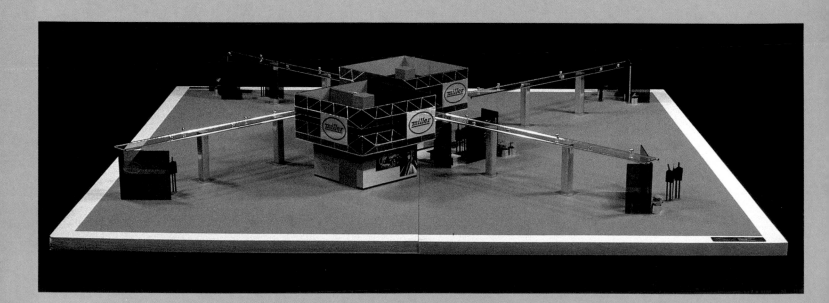

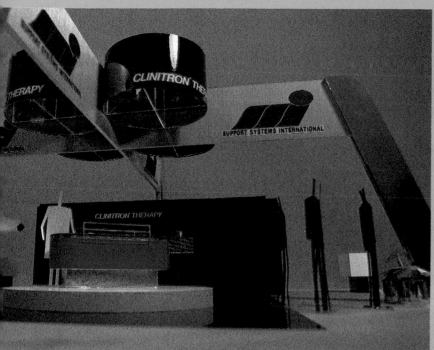

Exhibitor: Support Systems International
Designers: Richard Koplan, Dorothy Clark
Producer: Giltspur Exhibits/Pittsburgh,
               Pittsburgh, Pennsylvania

This two-level exhibit provides strong company identification, and areas for product demonstration and participation, as well as an area for private demonstrations and conferences. The pylons are engineered to be free standing during set-up.

226

Exhibitor: Mitsubishi
Designer: Stuart Stone
Producer: George P. Johnson Company, Warren, Michigan

Four 12 ft. brushed aluminum and plexiglass modules were used in the corners of this exhibit, giving both corporate and model identification. A large center unit was made with the same materials and design feeling.

Exhibitor: U.S. Steel
Designer: Don Graeb
Producer: Creative Productions, Pittsburgh,
              Pennsylvania

Angled pyramids symbolized the majesty of the corporation, while presenting information about three major divisions.

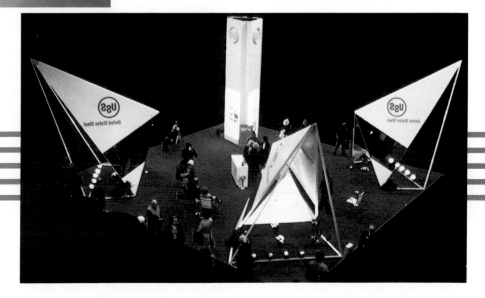

228

Exhibitor: 3M Corporation
Designer: Various
Producer: 3M Exhibit Facility, St. Paul, Minnesota

This exhibitor, represented by many divisions, participates in many shows. To make it possible for divisions to come together in various combinations, and yet to be able to exhibit successfully by themselves, the company has developed a standard corporate exhibit system, which consists of a limited number of components, shown in the accompanying drawing. All components, including vertical walls, overhead grids, carpeted curved sections, and flat panels, are of identical construction and are interchangeable.

Cabinets, each with a built-in inquiry slot and box, are all the same size, and can be used individually or as multiple units. Lighting is provided by light bars that rest on top of the overhead grid.

Most of the graphics are mounted to the grid in the display shop, and shipped that way. At the show, the only assembly is to bolt adjoining sections together.

The original design and system was developed by Harvey Chandler, but the examples of the use of the system shown in the illustrations were designed by a number of individuals.

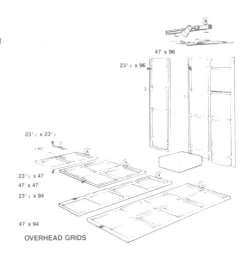

OVERHEAD GRIDS

Equipment Service
and Support

Service Network
Available to 3M
Customers

File Management Systems

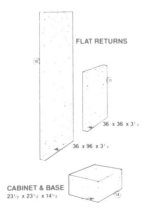

36 x 3½ x 2′ RADIUS
CURVED RETURNS

96 x 3½ x 2′ RADIUS

FLAT RETURNS

36 x 36 x 3½

36 x 96 x 3½

CABINET & BASE
23½ x 23½ x 14½

File
Management
Systems
Division

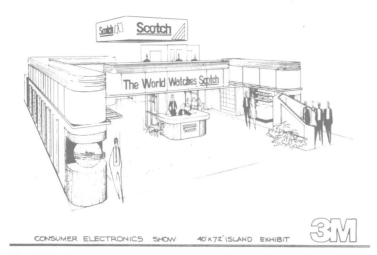

CONSUMER ELECTRONICS SHOW   40'x72' ISLAND EXHIBIT   **3M**

Exhibitor: 3M Corporation
Designer: Various
Producer: 3M Exhibit Facility, St. Paul, Minnesota

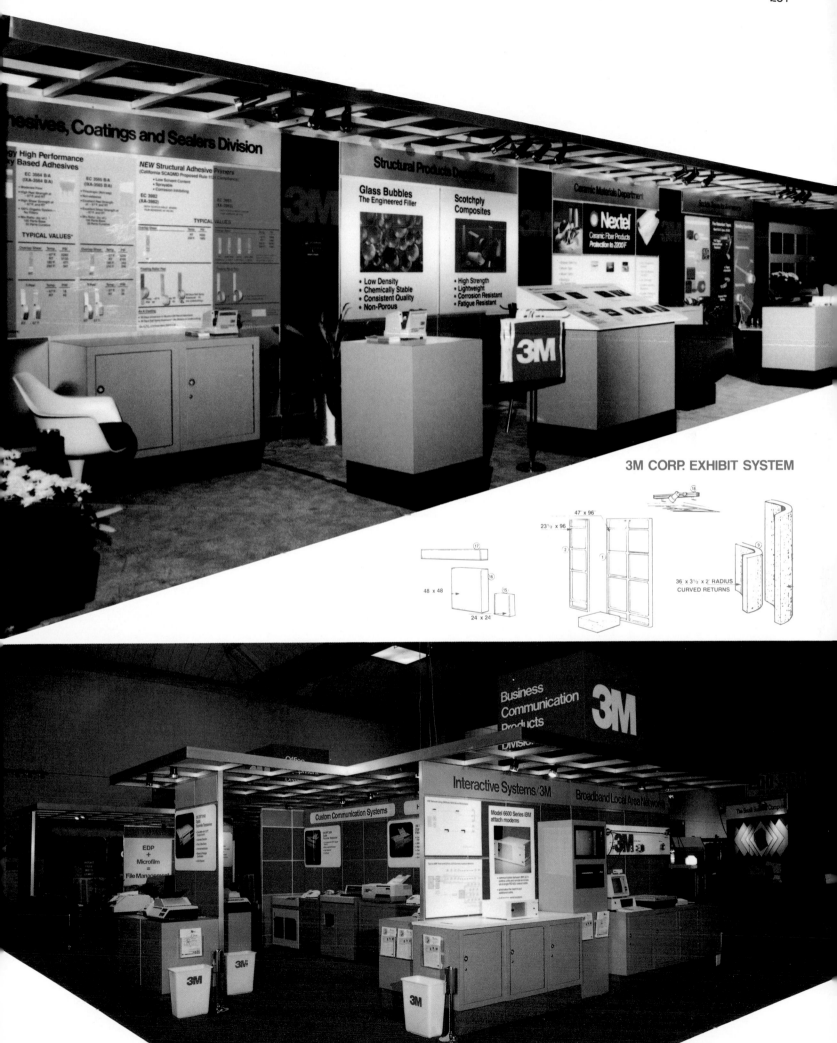

3M CORP. EXHIBIT SYSTEM

Exhibitor: Franklin Computer
Designer: Impact Exhibits, South Plainfield,
New Jersey
Producer: Impact Exhibits, South Plainfield,
New Jersey

Eighteen foot towers, with strong company identification, are designed into each corner of this exhibit. A central conference area has double entry and is enclosed with smoked plexiglass to provide a contemporary office environment.

Exhibitor: Surgikos
Designer: Dave Harbaugh
Producer: Giltspur Exhibits/Pittsburgh,
Pittsburgh, Pennsylvania

This double-decked exhibit used Meroform for the overhead treatment.

234

Exhibitor: General Electric Company
Designers: Tom Lemery, Gene Lindman, and Don Cooper
Producer: Global Exhibition Services, Brooklyn, New York

Occupying 9,000 sq. ft. at the International Machine Tool Show, this exhibit contained segments for a number of GE divisions. Each had to stand by itself and at the same time, be part of a coordinated whole. Most newsworthy was a television production stage and studio which offered live and taped pictures on a 46 in. diagonal screen and a live moderator. The bleachers held 102 people and about 50 more could watch the show on near-by monitors.

Another highlight was a fully operating manufacturing cell, utilizing five robots. For safety, bent plexi-railings, which came in units of 3 and 6 ft., let the audience get as close as possible, but kept them out of danger. The 8 × 28 ft. platform on which the robots were mounted was shipped on a single skid which permitted fast set-up.

Chapter **11**

New Ideas in Exhibit Design

The exhibit designer is more than an artist, engineer, educator, carpenter, and film producer. He's also a detective; he must constantly search for new materials and processes that will keep construction costs down without compromising the exhibit's effectiveness.

The rewards, such as those illustrated here, can be both fascinating and useful.

Want to simulate a fade or wipe, like those done on film, in real life? Now there's a plastic that changes from opaque to clear when electricity is applied. How about adding a Disneyesque quality to your exhibit with some talking money? Animatronic spokespersons are here, and just as effective in the commercial world as they have been in entertainment. Further developments in holography have made it viable for use in exhibits. The thin holographic films take up little space and can now be projected using widely available conventional bulbs under normal lighting conditions.

Designers are constantly under pressure to find more efficient materials—lighter, more effective, less expensive—and processes. But the exhibit designer has a handicap; trade publications serving the exhibit industry aren't a viable source of new information. Vendors of new materials regard the exhibit industry as a small market. Therefore, they make minimal efforts to reach exhibit designers, either through the trade press or through marketing programs.

As a result, designers have to track down new materials, design concepts, and interactive technologies in the trade press of other fields. Publications and trade shows geared to window displays, store decorations, packaging, and point of purchase materials can be good sources of new technology. Publications serving the audio-visual and photographic fields contain valuable information on new products.

The industries that produce construction materials—plastics, wood, and wood working machinery—are worth investigating.

Technical journals and trade shows for these fields may turn up useful materials. The designer may benefit from occasional reading of trade magazines in the hardware, housewares, architectural, and furniture design fields as well.

While compiling the materials for this book, wc received a number of submissions from companies which supply the exhibit industry. There are not whole exhibits, but rather processes or equipment to be used in exhibits—new tools available to designers. They are included here as clues in the on-going search for the perfect solution.

238

Designer: Bill Moss
Producer: Moss Design, Camden, Maine

These photos show the varied use of stretched canvas to attract attention, and enclose space economically. They can be used separately, making up the entire booth background, or they can be added on to existing exhibits as an inexpensive way of increasing area. They are used often as props, to control acoustical absorption, or as a projection screen.

Producer: ShowAmerica Inc., Elmhurst, Illinois

In addition to the robots of science fiction, robots can be made to look like a product package, or a trademarked character.

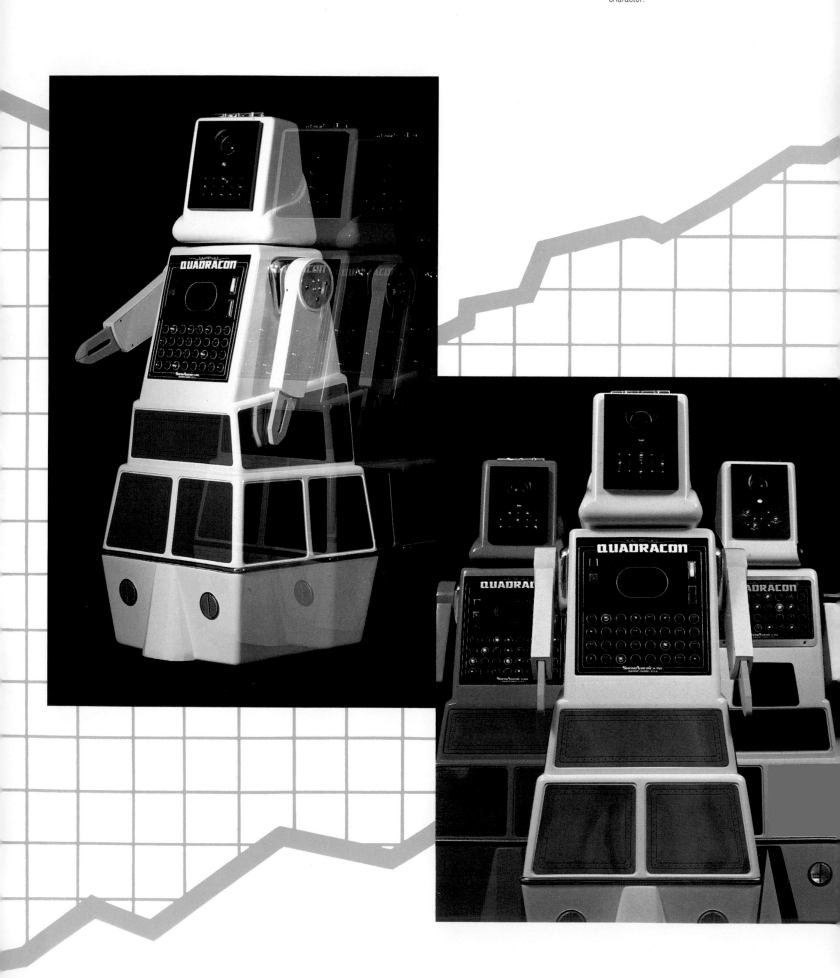

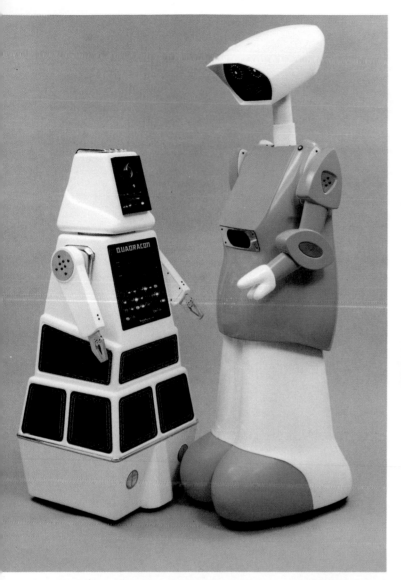

Exhibitor: NCR
Designer: Display Directions
Producer: 3M Commercial Graphics Division,
               St. Paul, Minnesota

It was a simple matter to turn a magazine ad into a panel which could be used in a display window, inside a store, or in an exhibit booth.

Exhibitor: Enterprise Square USA
Producer: Sally Animation Inc.,
              Jacksonville, Florida

Characters on currency come alive, talk, and sing about
the U.S. monetary system in this exhibit unit.

Producer: Frostee-Foam Company, Antioch, Illinois

A new process permits expanded polystyrene to be cut
accurately and automatically from an outline drawing.
This makes for economical reproduction of letters, logos,
products, pedestals, etc., on a one-time basis. The
light-weight material can be easily painted or laminated.

Exhibitor: McDonald's
Producer: Pallas Photo Labs Inc., Chicago, Illinois

The delicate variations of tone are easily captured in a large blow-up.

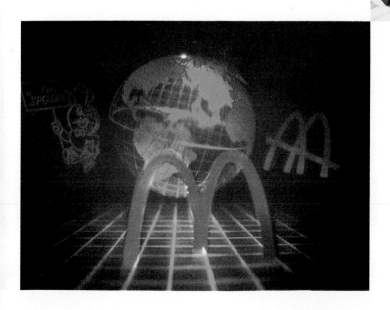

Exhibitor: McDonald's Corporation
Designer: Smith & Cvetkovich, Chicago, Illinois
Producer: Smith & Cvetkovich, Chicago, Illinois

For a permanent exhibit at corporate headquarters, a group of seven multi-color reflection holograms were produced. These holograms give an illusion of three dimensions, but take up little space, use easily-available bulbs, and can be viewed in normal lighting conditions.

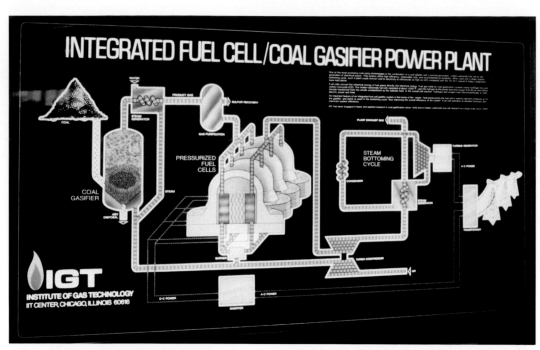

INTEGRATED FUEL CELL/COAL GASIFIER POWER PLANT

IGT
INSTITUTE OF GAS TECHNOLOGY
IIT CENTER, CHICAGO, ILLINOIS 60616

Exhibitor:	Institute of Gas Technology
Designers:	Ron Ferguson, Jack Winkler
Producer:	Exhibitgroup Chicago, Chicago, Illinois

These panels, illuminated from the rear, use continuous motion to illustrate the chemical process. The graphics are achieved by two large rotating wheels containing a polarizing film, driven in synch through a chain drive.

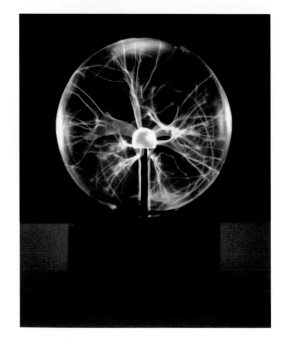

Producer:	Future Designs Inc., New York, New York

For a traffic-stopping item, consider one of these high-tech plasma-discharge sculptures, whose output is constantly changing, and even responds to the human touch. No two of these units are alike, and they possess a fascination that attracts people of all ages, all interests, and all educational levels.

Exhibitor: U.S. Air Force Recruiting Service
Designer: Walt Weibel

The entire display, including the structure, fits into the case seen in the picture.

Exhibitor: Brillion
Designer: Display Directions

The brilliant color of a hearth furnace is captured well by the Scanamural process.

Producer: Pallas Photo Labs, Inc., Chicago, Illinois

This Scanamural is an example of the details that can be incorporated into a large panel.

246

Exhibitor: Roche Laboratories
Designer: Global Exhibits
Producer: Electronic Exhibits, Inc.,
Englewood, New Jersey

One of the outstanding applications of electronics to
exhibitry was this tower with changeable panels, which
can display pre-installed messages as well as those
typed-in on the site. This is one of the techniques, based
on computer applications, developed by the producer.

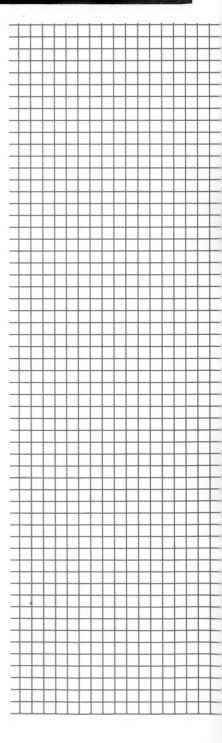

Producer: Graphic Systems, Minneapolis,
Minnesota

Lending new mobility to exhibits, this 6×8 ft. lightbox,
including lighting fixtures and transparency, fold down
into two carrying cases. The metal frame snaps out, and
the light fixtures are held in place with hooks. The
transparency is attached with Velcro.

Designer: Albin Kaut, Steinheim,
West Germany
Producer: Albin Kaut, Steinheim,
West Germany

For a quick backdrop or a free-standing background, this wall is made up of squares that attach to each other. Each square has interior illumination, with the power source in the horizontal base unit.

Designer: Roctronics Lighting, Pembroke,
Massachusetts
Producer: Roctronics Lighting, Pembroke,
Massachusetts

For an unusual method of attracting attention, you might use an element that involves some of the most advanced techniques of light control, including fog, bubbles, stroboscopes, ultraviolet, or laser beams. In the effect illustrated, the display behind the girl can spin, explode, and change color in tempo to music or to voice.

Producer: Taliq, Mountain View, California

These sheets of plastic can change in a millisecond from opaque to clear with an application of a small electric current. It's a fascinating effect, and by programming a series of switches, a developing story or visual effect may be achieved.

Appendix

ASPECTS OF EXHIBIT DESIGN ESSAYS

The Role of the Independent Designer

by Ralph LaZar, IDSA
Herbst, LaZar, Rogers & Bell, Inc.
Chicago, Illinois

As an independent designer working in many fields, I find exhibit design especially unique. Exhibit designers have the opportunity of creating a complete world or environment for the viewer. The designer's primary task is to devise the most effective way of communicating the exhibit's message to the viewer. This design experience is exciting, engrossing—sometimes frustrating— and very rewarding.

Exhibits come in all types and sizes; from trade show booths to museum displays, corporate showroom exhibits to world's fair pavillions. Regardless of the type or size, success is determined by how faithfully the designer adheres to a workable design methodology. The first step, and probably most important, is orientation to the project. The designer must take the time to thoroughly understand the client and the message that is to be communicated.

Orientation meetings between the design team and the client's management and technical staffs should be set to discuss the objectives and the parameters of the exhibit. In developing a corporate exhibit, the marketing department may be concerned with the need to display products; engineers may stress the importance of manufacturing techniques and product features; management may want to portray the company's history and project its future market position. Interaction between the designer's and client's staffs can help establish priorities.

Once the image of the company that is to be portrayed is determined, other criteria, such as the nature of the audience, the size, and budgets should be discussed.

The next step is for the designers to generate conceptual ideas and portray them in sketches, models, or storyboards. Appropriate exhibit techniques, such as interactive hands-on displays, film presentations, videos, demonstration models, graphics, music, sound, and live performances should be examined.

When the purpose, size, and contents of an exhibit have been decided, the designer must create a custom exhibit structure or select a stock system.

The next phase of design is to thoroughly document the exhibit and its contents. Detailed drawings, layouts, space plans, and electrical plans are made. Finished art is produced and photo image selections are made. All of the specifications, including type, text placement, materials, finishes, and color specifications are completed.

This material is then distributed to a number of selected exhibit fabricators who then submit estimates for the cost of completing the project. Many designers—and clients—make the mistake of thinking that the design effort is finished when the construction contracts are signed.

Some contingencies are difficult, if not impossible, to anticipate during design. The designer has to be available for final approval of finishes, colors, or items that have to be substituted if the originals can't be obtained.

The designer should remain involved through the installation phase; even here some changes may be necessary and the designer should review a staging of the exhibit at the fabricator's shop.

Exhibit design is an interdisciplinary activity calling for a wide range of design skills. There is no ideal form for an exhibit. No matter what approach is taken, the design must be applied to the form, and the design components must be consistent, cohesive, and unified within the form. Final success is judged by the interest, excitement, and enthusiasm demonstrated by the show attendee. The exaltation the designer feels when seeing the exhibit in finished form can only be exceeded by the knowledge that the client's goals have been fulfilled.

Designing for the United Kingdom and Europe

by Brian A. Ward
Managing Director
Newton Display Group, Ltd.
Manchester, England

There are considerable differences in designing for trade show exhibitions in the United States and designing for exhibitions on the eastern side of the Atlantic Ocean. Not only are different construction methods used, but the whole scale of distances and, therefore, transport of exhibits are far different. London, for example, is closer to Paris, than it is to Glasgow, Scotland; and Moscow is closer to England than Chicago is to San Francisco. Moreover, Europe has excellent highways. This has led to the custom of contractors building an exhibit, then transporting, erecting, and dismantling it in a number of successive cities. While some local assistance may be required, the contractor will almost always maintain control and supervise the process. How different this is from the United States, where transportation and construction are often delegated to shipping firms and on-site contractors. For American companies exhibiting in Europe, the tighter control afforded by the European system can help overcome the worries of having to deal with the profusion of languages and customs on the Continent.

Similarly, there are basic differences between common practice in the United States and Europe with regard to the special needs of shell-scheme interiors, single-deck free space stands, double-deck free space stands, and outdoor sites.

Shell-Scheme Interiors

Unlike the United States, where only carpet and drapes are supplied by the exhibition hall, many European shows also supply solid rear and side walls of a neutral color, a fascia with a sign giving the exhibitor's name and stand number, and a ceiling. These pre-fab exhibits are called shells, and may also include electrical outlets, tables and chairs, counters, storage cabinets, shelves for supplies, and display panels.

The walls and ceilings of these shells are generally from one of the widely available modular display systems. Designers accustomed to working with these shells often utilize the supplied walls, painting them or covering them with material. Custom display panels, lights, and other features can generally be locked into the aluminum frames supplied with the shells.

Single-Deck Free Space Stands

A free space stand is simply an area of floor space on which exhibitors are free to build their own structures. The exhibitor is free to choose any contractor to build the display, and is not obligated to use one particular contractor supplied by the exhibition sponsor.

"Single-deck" means that the exhibit is one level, and doesn't have a second story, although it may have a series of raised platforms.

In the United States, exhibits are generally designed so that they can be disassembled for shipment and reassembled for future use. In Europe, many exhibits are designed for one-time use only. The designer, therefore, has more flexibility, and the contractor may use stock structural items to achieve economies.

When an exhibitor contracts with a show sponsor for a "single-deck" stand, the height is not usually restricted, as it is if the exhibitor rents a shell exhibit with a ceiling. The use of towers, spires, or other displays is common, but check to ensure that the show regulations permit them.

Double-Deck Free Space Stands

Where space is at a premium, it's common to use a structure with a second floor. The second floor is often devoted to private discussion areas, offices, refreshment areas, or storage.

Although this type of construction is expensive, and must conform to strict local safety regulations, when the cost of ground space in an exhibit hall is considered, it can be very cost-effective and enhance the exhibit's impact.

Outdoor Sites

Outdoor exhibitions play a major part in some industries; in the United Kingdom, agricultural shows and similar outdoor events account for about a fifth of all spending on exhibitions.

Sites at outdoor shows may be within open-front tents or they may be completely free-standing designs. Due to the unpredictability of weather, most outdoor shows are mounted during the summer months, and even then, the design has to allow for the possibility of high wind and rain

Generally, these shows tend to be held annually on permanent sites, and many of the stands are permanent structures which are left unused during most of the year. For the next use, a thorough cleaning, a new coat of paint, and new graphics put the exhibitors in business for another year. The open-front canvas tent is the basic shell at most outdoor shows, and this does keep off the worst of the rain. It's difficult to design an exciting booth inside a tent, but the use of signs and towers outside or over the tent can enhance the exhibit.

Some exhibitors who attend a number of outdoor shows equip a mobile trailer which can be driven onto an open site. With the sides opened, signs installed and electricity installed, it is ready for business very quickly.

Materials and Standards

There seems to be a greater use of lighter materials in Europe, where short-term use is required, with less emphasis on the strength needed for a reusable display.

For American companies exhibiting in Europe, it may be useful to employ a European design firm, or, alternatively, to produce the exhibit concept and then get advice on adapting the ideas to the local conditions and materials.

In particular, United States companies should be aware of the differences in measurements—almost always in metric units—and in electrical standards. The characteristics of electrical current and the design of electrical connectors not only differ when you cross the Atlantic, they vary greatly from country to country.

Special Considerations for the Exhibit Designer

by ROBERT FIRKS, President
Giltspur Exhibits, Chicago, Illinois
Past President, Exhibit Designers and
Producers Association

The purpose of an exhibit is to lure passersby from nearby exhibit booths, showcase products, convey the company's image and educate show attendees about new products, technological breakthroughs or other industry developments. A successful design is more than a cluster of modules, eye-catching graphics, exciting product demonstrations and colorful visuals. Effective exhibit design is the sum of all the creativity, hands-on experience, marketing knowledge and salesmanship that can be brought to bear on the subject.

The design process begins with a thorough definition of the client's marketing objectives. A thorough information-gathering process will aid the designer in creating a design that balances marketing objectives and stimulating graphics. What product, service, idea or concept does the exhibitor want to promote? How does the exhibitor define its market position? How does this corporate or product image fare against its competitors? What, specifically, are the exhibitor's sales goals? Will the personnel and staff play a major role in serving the exhibitor's marketing objectives?

Without well-defined objectives, an in-depth knowledge of the exhibitor's products and services, as well as its image within the marketplace, it will be difficult for the designer to create an attractive display that furthers the client's marketing position, supports its marketing objectives, and informs show attendees of the unique products or services available.

Keeping in mind the exhibitor's marketing objectives, the designer's next step involves conceptualizing the design. How should the message be communicated? What design elements will engage passersby? What structural materials would best convey the exhibitor's marketing concept? Does the client have existing props that could be altered, or does the designer need to create new fixtures? Is the exhibit space large enough to accommodate the necessary fixtures and still leave enough room for customers?

Once these questions are answered, the designer is ready to begin shaping the exhibit. Exhibit design has not been refined to a science; there

are few boundaries and limitations. In seeking a fresh design approach, the designer should study techniques used successfully by others in serving an exhibitor's marketing objectives while, at the same time, drawing attention away from competitors.

The exhibit designer must understand how scale and balance contribute to a professional, inviting exhibit space. Thoughtful design and layout take into consideration traffic flow; highlighting points of interest; mixing, matching colors for a visual impact; and choosing fixtures and props that accent, rather than detract from, the desired effect.

Show attendance and the size of the exhibit space will determine, to a large extent, how the floor plan is designed and the type of fixtures that are chosen. If large crowds are expected, the designer may consider an open, airy floor plan that allows easy movement through the exhibit space.

According to research, the designer should plan approximately 25 square feet of space per person. The positioning of fixtures should not inhibit traffic flow. Knowing how to scale height and width, when to use large or small patterns, how to select textures and when to choose light or dark colors, all are important design considerations.

In choosing colors and textures, the basic design principles apply: light colors and shiny, reflecting surfaces visually expand space. Geometric and diagonal patterns appear to push out and extend walls and floors. By contrast, dark colors and soft, matte surfaces make a space seem smaller. The same is true of large, bold patterns. The designer should choose colors, textures and patterns that best convey the exhibitor's image to his defined audience.

Lighting is another design element that, if used properly, can accentuate the exhibitor's products and image. Color temperature indicates the relative amount of light emitted in the two basic color ranges—warm and cool. Warm lights emit more red, orange and yellow, while cool lights emit more green, blue and violet. The higher the color temperature, the cooler—or more blue—

the light. Warm lights impart a homey atmosphere. Cooler light, such as warm-white fluorescent, may display the colors of product packages more accurately in a main sales area. Lighting, whether warm or cool, indirect or direct, should be chosen to create an effect.

While the designer may want to spend the most time creating efficient floor plans, designing fixtures and choosing color schemes, he must pay careful attention to the budget. The choice of materials, construction techniques and methods of transporting the exhibit all are standard budget items. But the designer should also consider the use—and cost—of printed promotion, signage, graphics, personnel, and audio visual and other equipment for demonstration areas. While not the major responsibility of the designer, these "accessories" must be figured into the budget, for they are often the finishing touches of a well-designed exhibit.

A cost-conscious designer is one who respects the exhibitor's desire for adequate return-on-investment and diligently seeks new and inexpensive design techniques without compromising the exhibitor's marketing objectives. Exhibit design is ever-changing. New challenges, and opportunities, arise with every project. As long as there is a need for innovative ways to charm, delight, inform, and achieve results through exhibit design, there will always be an abundance of design solutions.

Museum Exhibits: A Fusion of History and Sales

by Nicholas B. Paffett
Krent/Paffett Associates
Boston, Massachusetts

What do industry trade shows and museum exhibits have in common? They both sell. Trade show exhibitors promote products and services to a target audience through high-power sales techniques: offers the show-goer can't refuse, products that will give his business a competitive edge, and new ways to do business. Designing the trade show exhibit demands state-of-the-art techniques that will lure passersby away from competitors.

Designers of museum exhibits don't have the advantage of selling a group of people who share common interests, business skills, and knowledge. The museum exhibit doesn't sell products or services; it conveys information to people with diverse backgrounds who are seeking to add knowledge, quality, and entertainment to their lives. Museums strive to enrich a visitor's life in unique ways. Where else can people watch a world-renowned impressionist paint or see a 19th-century waterwheel or the toothsome surface of a coral reef? Museums offer experiences that most people can't create for themselves. The designer must meet the challenges of its diverse audience, complex subject matter and limited budgets through careful planning and thoughtful design.

In conceiving a museum exhibit, the designer is part of a three-person team, including a scientist and scholar. Often, the museum's board of directors will solicit the expertise of others researchers, writers, behavioral scientists, and information specialists. In working with these experts, the designer must assume the role of a creative educator seeking to entertain, inform, and involve the visitor. Display objects don't tell the whole tale; they're merely a part of a larger story that must be unfolded. The designer must weave artifacts as if they were the fabric of a story, concept, or process. A successful museum exhibit designer is one who possesses the analytical skills to combine artifacts and assemble historical data into an informative presentation.

It's all too possible for the medium to become the message. The designer must maintain control of the design vehicle, making sure that it doesn't overpower the message. He must adhere to the educational goals and written program established by the museum's board of directors. Abstract and complex ideas should be conveyed in a simple, fun, and understandable way. One successful approach is known as spiral learning —ideas unfold one at a time to enable the visitor to digest complicated information in bite-size pieces.

Just as trade show exhibits require careful planning, so do museum exhibits. The designer must understand the museum's philosophy, its program, the demographic makeup of its visitors, and budget restrictions. Every artifact and graphic must be carefully selected. Information must be well-articulated and presented in a simple, understandable fashion. Limited budgets often make it impossible for the museum to replace exhibits frequently. Therefore, the exhibit must be durable and be able to effectively communicate for five years, ten years or longer.

Budgets, security, time and available talent all play a critical role in the success of a museum exhibit. Electronic and mechanical devices can increase design and construction costs substantially. Mechanical failures and faulty equipment can decrease the life expectancy of the exhibit. Electronic and mechanical devices can be costly, too. A graphic panel may be less expensive to produce and maintain than a 16mm film or a Van de Graaff electrostatic generator. However, the visitor may retain the information that's presented by a 16mm film or a lighting show longer than they would information contained in a graphic.

Museum design is both challenging and rewarding. If properly planned and designed, the museum display can convey useful information and continue making an impact on visitors for many years—or even many generations.

Audio-Visual Presentations: On with the Show

by Arthur L. Friedman
President
General Exhibits, Inc.
Philadelphia, Pennsylvania

Imagine that you've been commissioned to design an exhibit for the manufacturer of catamarans. Limitations of budget and exhibit space don't allow you to display the sleek, swift vessel. But the client still hopes to tantalize passersby with the excitement of banking off of a northeast wind and skipping through the surf. For some exhibitors, an audio-visual presentation is the next best thing to being there.

A dynamic and carefully planned audio-visual presentation—whether a 16mm film, videotape, videodisc, or multi-projector slide show—can mean the difference between brisk business and an empty exhibit booth. An exciting, action-packed presentation can deliver an enormous amount of information in a relatively short period of time, create a lasting impression, and even reduce the number of personnel needed to staff the exhibit booth. Perhaps more important, a well-designed audio-visual presentation can command the attention of potential clients who might otherwise be enticed to shop your competitors.

Budget considerations often decide the type of audio-visual presentation used, but there are other important factors that must be considered by the designer:

- *Time*: The presentation must be long enough to convey key selling points, but not so long that the visitor loses interest in the presentation and the exhibitor's product.

- *Media*: Select the medium, or a combination of media, that effectively showcase the exhibitor's product, keeping in mind the size of the booth and the exhibitor's marketing objectives. Films create perhaps the best impression at trade shows, but they can be expensive and difficult to produce. Motion pictures are usually reserved for audiences of 100 or more people. Videotapes, on the other hand, are less expensive to produce. Half-inch video equipment permits seven hours of continuous viewing on a single cassette. And the images are generally crisp and clear.

- *Environment*: Make sure that the exhibit space is large enough for easy viewing and listening. There's nothing more irritating to a prospective client than straining to hear or see the show, whether on a television monitor or a 30-foot screen.

Not all products or services lend themselves to audio-visual presentations. The best candidates are those products which involve some action but which, for practical purposes, cannot be brought into the exhibit hall. An automobile manufacturer who wants to showcase a new line of sports cars can easily display the newest models for all to admire. But if the goal is to promote the company's state-of-the-art engineering, a 16mm film may do a better job than a complex verbal sales presentation.

Motion may also be simulated using two or more projectors; in addition, multiplexers now make it possible to transfer the multiple images from a number of projectors to a single 16mm film or videotape. This reduces the amount of hardware needed to display the presentation to a single projector or video cassette recorder.

Audio visual presentations that allow viewer interaction are becoming more popular. Interactive displays allow visitors to access information at their own pace, and to retrieve the specific information they're interested in from a large mass of general data. Videodisc players and less expensive disc mastering has made building interactive displays easier. The videodisc, which allows for random access to the recorded material, can be controlled by a microcomputer or a touch panel activated by the viewer. The microcomputer can be used to control a user-directed simulation of the action of an earth mover, for example. And the computer can record visitor reactions, thus enhancing the gathering of marketing information.

After the appropriate medium is determined, it is important to provide the right environment for the presentation. It should be located in an area isolated from the distracting traffic, noise, and activity of a trade show. The optimum setting is a properly-designed theater.

The ideal theater is rare at trade shows. The cost—perhaps up to $100,000—and size, up to 900 square feet, make it prohibitive for most exhibitors.

All good theaters, however, share some characteristics. A structure that has two walls of smoked plexiglass fronting on show aisles permits passersby to see that something is going on inside, yet light levels inside are low enough for proper viewing. A ceiling of black acoustical fiberglass can be used to eliminate light from above. Draped or sound-proofed walls keep the presentation's audio track from distracting visitors outside the theater and keep exterior noises from disturbing the viewers inside. Small lights on the backs of chairs help visitors take notes.

The sophistication of audio visual presentations is increasing rapidly. New technology, particularly video and small computers, are reducing the cost of production while making the presentations more responsive to viewer needs. A Sony videotape unit interfaced with a microcomputer now allows the viewer to not only select the information presented, but to receive a printed hard copy of the data. Indeed, it is not inconceiveable that techniques rarely used today will soon be common, and that some of the most sophisticated equipment will soon be made obsolete by new technology.

Index

Exhibitors

DESIGNERS